MW00460942

S*The*enate Prayers
P*of*eter Marshall

S*The*enate Prayers
Peter *of* Marshall

with a Retrospective by
the Rev. Lloyd Ogilvie
Chaplain, U.S. Senate

CHAPMAN BILLIES, INC.
SANDWICH MA

This edition published in 1997 by
Chapman Billies, Inc.
Box 819, Sandwich, MA 02563.

Manufactured in the United States of America

Production supervised by Jenna Dixon

ISBN 0-939218-11-9

Publisher's Cataloging in Publication
  (prepared by Quality Books, Inc.)
Marshall, Peter, 1902–1949.
    The Senate prayers of Peter Marshall : delivered at the
opening of the daily sessions of the Senate of the United
States during the Eightieth and Eighty-first Congresses,
1947–1949 / with a retrospective by Lloyd Ogilvie.
      p.   cm.
    ISBN 0-939218-11-9
    1. Legislative bodies—Chaplain's prayers. 2. United
States. Congress. Senate. I. Title.
    BV280.M37 1996
    242.8'8   QBI96-20202

Resolved, That Reverend Peter Marshall, Doctor of Divinity, of the District of Columbia, be, and he is hereby, elected Chaplain of the Senate.

—Senate Resolution No. 10
Eightieth Congress, First Session
(Submitted by Mr. Wherry)
In the Senate of the United States
Attest: Carl A. Loeffler, Secretary
JANUARY 4, 1947

Resolved by the Senate (the House of Representatives concurring), That there be printed as a Senate document, the prayers offered by the Chaplain, the Reverend Peter Marshall, Doctor of Divinity, at the opening of the daily sessions of the Senate of the United States during the Eightieth Congress, 1947-1948, and at the opening of the first ten daily sessions of the Senate of the United States, Eighty-first Congress, 1949, together with excerpts from the Congressional Record relative to Doctor Marshall's death; and that six thousand additional copies be printed and bound, of which five thousand shall be for the use of the Senate and one thousand shall be for the use of the Joint Committee on Printing.

—Senate Concurrent Resolution No. 19
Eighty-first Congress
(Submitted by Mr. Gurney)
In the Senate of the United States
FEBRUARY 25 (LEGISLATIVE DAY,
FEBRUARY 21), 1949
ADOPTED JUNE 15, 1949

FOREWORD

Rev. Peter Marshall was Chaplain of the Senate for two years while I presided as president pro tempore in the absence of a Vice President. Thus it was my daily privilege to greet him each noon when the Senate convened and to present him to my colleagues for his daily prayer. This duty swiftly became a precious privilege for me and this routine quickly became an inspiration. My Chaplain became my intimate and priceless friend.

Dr. Marshall was a rugged Christian with dynamic faith. He was an eloquent and relentless crusader for righteousness in the lives of men and nations. He always spoke with courage, with deepest human understanding, and with stimulating hope. To know him was to love him. His sudden and untimely death was a loss of major magnitude to countless friends in whose hearts his memory will long and vividly survive.

I count it a rare privilege to be permitted this foreword to a reprint of his Senate prayers.

HON. ARTHUR H. VANDENBERG
U.S. Senator from Michigan

PREFACE

You are about to begin an exciting adventure of intercessory prayer with one of the truly great spiritual leaders of the twentieth century. Guided by the eloquent prayers of Dr. Peter Marshall, the fifty-fourth Chaplain of the United States Senate, you will be able to fulfill the biblical admonition to pray for our nation and its leaders. You will find these prayers will assist you in articulating your own prayers about the soul-sized issues and problems we face today. This little book will become an invaluable companion in your high calling as an intercessor for God's best for our land. You will find that the depth and vision of your prayers for leaders will increase day by day.

Peter Marshall was pastor of the New York Avenue Presbyterian Church in Washington, D.C., when he was elected to be the Chaplain of the Senate in January 1947. His dynamic preaching had drawn several of the senators to his historic church. Republican Majority Whip Kenneth Wherry of Nebraska, a faithful follower of Dr. Marshall's preaching, made the recommendation to the Republican conference and subsequently extended the invitation to Peter Marshall.

Since the Chaplaincy then was not a full-time position, the duties would have to be added to the pastor's already full and demanding schedule. The Chaplain of the Senate was responsible not only for the opening prayer, but also to serve as pastoral advisor to the senators, their families, and staffs.

After extended prayer about the opportunity, he received a clarion call from the Lord to accept the position. On January 4, 1947, he was elected by a majority of the Senate.

Senate historians remind us that Dr. Marshall's election had been embroiled in party politics and that the Senate he was called to serve had not been unanimous in his election. The newly empowered Republican majority of the Eightieth Congress, as part of the changing of the guard, proposed him over the objection of some in the Democratic minority who wanted to keep in the post of Chaplain Dr. Frederick Harris, a fellow pastor and friend of Peter Marshall. Research of the Washington Evening Star of January 4, 1947, reveals this headline: "Dr. Peter Marshall Elected Chaplain After Party Fight, Senate Democrats Lose Move To Keep Dr. Harris in Post." Dr. Marshall was troubled by this partisan battle and knew that he had a challenge ahead of him to be a non-partisan Chaplain winning over those who had lost in the political maneuvering surrounding his election.

It was not long, however, until both Democrats and Republicans became staunch supporters of their new Chaplain. His powerful prayers and strong leadership were affirmed two years later when he was reelected by the Democratic Senate majority of the Eighty-First Congress. He served until his untimely death on January 27, 1949, just two years and twenty-three days after his first election.

Peter Marshall brought to the Chaplaincy the magnificent combination of his ruddy Scot's character and his robust faith, his lilting Scot's burr and his zest for life. His relationship with God had been nurtured by a virile Scottish heritage and a dramatic encounter with God. Through the years his prayer life had grown in intimacy and integrity. His prayers reveal both his awe and wonder before God and his belief that God really cares about the down-to-earth problems and perplexities of daily life.

Praying with Peter Marshall the prayers he prayed in his short tenure as Chaplain of the Senate becomes an inspiring training experience in how to be an effective intercessor for the nation and its leaders. We are introduced to the God who seeks to bless our country. All these prayers communicate a deep trust in God's sovereignty. We are taught how to talk simply and forthrightly to God about the needs of the nation. Also, these prayers give us a sense of the empathy and compassion required really to intercede for strategic leaders. We feel Peter Marshall's profound love for the senators for whom he prayed. He was concerned for their relationship with God and one another, their health and inner happiness, their joys and sorrows. Each of the prayers also ends with a liberating commitment to God as the only source of freedom from debilitating anxiety and fear.

It is obvious that Dr. Marshall deeply respected the talent, training, and experience of the senators. However, he was aware that leading this nation required supernatural power. He constantly led the senators in a humble prayer for the anointing of the Spirit with the gifts of wisdom, discernment, and vision. No one can read these prayers without a renewed sense of his or her own need for the Lord to empower beyond the limits of human adequacy.

When Peter Marshall began the Senate Chaplaincy, he was used to praying his carefully thought-out prayers without a written script or notes. He felt this gave him greater freedom to talk to God as one talks to a friend without pretension or studied rhetoric. He soon was told that the Congressional Record required a written copy of his prayer prior to the delivery at the opening of the Senate. This presented quite a problem for Marshall. Then he discovered that the long period of preparation of the written text provided God access to his mind and heart in an even deeper way than in his usual extemporaneous method. We are thankful; Marshall's magnificent prayers were preserved for us.

Dr. Marshall's skill as a wordsmith is revealed in the written manuscripts of his sermons. He was a master of the metaphor as he drew his impelling word pictures to help people grasp the truth. The discipline of writing his prayers for the Senate brought forth the same penetrating thought expressed in pithy wording. His words lingered in the Senatorial memory long after they were heard. As Senator Scott W. Lucas put it, "While he had no voice in determining policy and had no vote on any measure that came before us, his prayers carried weight in our hearts and many times moved us in the right direction." And Senator Estes Kefauver expressed gratitude for the empathy from their Chaplain he and other senators felt when they heard Marshall's compassionate prayers. "As a man above politics," Kefauver said, "he bowed to the needs and desires of this body. Would that God give all of us here in the Senate the strength and the courage to live up to his simple, provocative, yet easily understood prayers."

Peter Marshall never used his prayers as a "bully pulpit" to preach to the senators. So often what masquerades as authentic intercessory prayer for the nation's leaders is either telling God what He should do or instructing the leaders on what we think God wants them to do.

Marshall dealt with the spiritual issues and character proclivities that often make all of us less than effective. Many of his prayers confronted the debilitating influences of pride, arrogance, and selfishness that rob us of greatness in the battle for righteousness and justice in the nation. In Marshall's prayers, we hear the outspoken pleas to God of the Old Testament prophets, the yearning love of the Suffering Servant and the apostolic intensity of a Paul or John. Most important of all, here was a Chaplain who dared talk to God heart-to-heart with absolute confidence that his prayers had originated from Him and would be answered.

Added to all this, these prayers give us a fresh burst of unashamed patriotism. Peter Marshall loved this land that had adopted him as a cherished son. He never took for granted blessings God had lavished on this nation or the freedom given us in the Bill of Rights and the Constitution. His prayer about liberty rings with reality, "Teach us that liberty is not only to be loved but lived. Liberty is too precious a thing to be buried in books. It costs too much to be hoarded. Make us to see that liberty is not the right to do as we please, but the opportunity to please to do what is right."

You will note that all of these prayers are brief. Some are but a short paragraph of a few sentences. Peter Marshall never exceeded the two minute limit for prayers opening the Senate. He believed that the effectiveness of his prayers was in reverse ratio to their length. Often, the more pointed the theme of the prayer, the more brief was the length of the prayer. The Senate never suffered from a ho-hum, here we go again, at length, repetition of long, wordy prayers.

The reflections of Senator Arthur H. Vandenberg, president pro tempore of the Senate for the two years of Marshall's Chaplaincy, provide a moving testimony of the receptivity of political leaders to authentic spiritual inspiration:

> It was my daily privilege to meet the Chaplain each noon
> when the Senate convened and to present him to my col-

leagues for his daily prayer. This duty swiftly became a precious privilege for me and this routine quickly became an inspiration. My Chaplain became my intimate and priceless friend.

Dr. Marshall was a rugged Christian with dynamic faith. He was an eloquent and relentless crusader for righteousness in the lives of men and nations. He always spoke with courage, with deep human understanding, and with stimulating hope. To know him was to love him.

Senator Vandenberg's words took on great significance to me personally when I was elected to be the sixty-first Chaplain to the Senate. They became part of a mission vision, a hope, and a goal because they defined the role of a truly effective intercessor involved in a faith relationship with the God to whom he prayed and a trust relationship with the people for whom he prayed. No finer accolade could be given to a Chaplain of the Senate.

Now it is time for you to claim your rebirthed right to intercede for local, state, and national leaders. Peter Marshall's prayers will stretch your thinking and loosen your tongue as you discover how to put into your own words the prayers that will claim God's destiny for our beloved nation.

LLOYD JOHN OGILVIE
61st Chaplain
United States Senate

S*The*enate P*r*ayers
P*of*eter Marshall

EIGHTIETH CONGRESS
FIRST SESSION

O LORD OUR GOD if ever we needed Thy wisdom and Thy guidance, it is now—as the Congress begins a new session, standing upon the threshold of a new year, fraught with so many dangerous opportunities. We pray that Thou wilt bless these men chosen by the people of this nation, for Thou knowest them, their needs, their motives, their hopes, and their fears. Lord Jesus, put Thine arm around them to give them strength, and speak to them to give them wisdom greater than their own. May they hear Thy voice, and seek Thy guidance. May they remember that Thou art concerned about what is said and done here, and may they have clear conscience before Thee, that they need fear no man. Bless each of us according to our deepest need, and use us for Thy glory, we humbly ask in Jesus' name.

MONDAY, JANUARY 6, 1947

ETERNAL FATHER of our souls, grant to the members and the officers of this body a sacred moment of quiet ere they take up the duties of the day. Turn their thoughts to Thee, and open their hearts to Thy Spirit, that they may have wisdom in their decisions, understanding in their thinking, love in their attitudes, and mercy in their judgments.

Let them not think, when prayer is said, that their dependence upon Thee is over, and forget Thy counsels for the rest of the day.

Rather from these moments of heart-searching may there come such a sweetness of disposition that all may know that Thou art in this place. From this holy interlude may there flow a light and joy and power that will remain with them until night shall bring Thy whispered benediction, "Well done, good and faithful servant."

So help us all this day, through Jesus Christ our Lord. Amen. WEDNESDAY, JANUARY 8, 1947

LORD JESUS, Thou hast promised to give us the Holy Spirit if we are willing to open our hearts and let Him in. Make us willing now that things of eternal significance may begin to happen here. We know deep down in our hearts that without Thy guidance we can do nothing, but with Thee we can do all things. Let us not be frightened by the problems that confront us, but rather give Thee thanks that Thou hast matched us with this hour. May we resolve, God helping us, to be part of the answer, and not part of the problem.

For Jesus' sake. Amen. FRIDAY, JANUARY 10, 1947

SAVE THIS MOMENT, O Lord, from being merely a gesture to custom or convention, and make it a real experience for each one of us in this place, as we call upon Thee for guidance and for help.

We have felt Thee near and beside us in the exalted experience of worship in church; make us now to feel Thy nearness in the business of the day—the Unseen Delegate, present and voting. Vote through these men, we pray Thee, O Jesus, that what they say and what they do may be in accordance with Thy will for this land that we love so much.

Thou hast said: "When ye stand praying, forgive, if ye have aught against any." Give us the grace to lay aside all bitterness or resentment we may be nursing in our hearts, lest their acid eat into our peace and corrode our spirits.

Thou hast said: "It is more blessed to give than to receive." Give us the grace today to think not of what we can get but of what we can give, that a new spirit may come into our work here, with a new vision and a new purpose, that Thou wilt delight to bless.

We ask these things in Thine own name and for Thy sake. Amen.　　　　　　　　　MONDAY, JANUARY 13, 1947

OUR FATHER who art in heaven, we acknowledge that Thou dost govern in the affairs of men. And if a sparrow cannot fall to the ground without Thy notice, how can we think Thou art indifferent to what we say and do here?

If this day Thou dost want us to do, or not to do, any particular thing, we pray that Thou wilt make it plain to us, for Thou knowest how blind we can be, and how stubborn, in our own intentions. We pray for Thy help in our thinking and Thy love in our hearts. Through Jesus Christ our Lord. Amen.　　　　　　　　　WEDNESDAY, JANUARY 15, 1947

O LORD OUR GOD, before whom one day we shall all have to give account, lend us Thine aid, that this day's work may be well pleasing unto Thee.

If there be any here sulking as children will, deal with and enlighten him. Make it day about that person, so that he shall see himself and be ashamed. Make it heaven about him, Lord, by the only way to heaven, forgetfulness of self, and

5

make it day about his neighbors, so that they shall help and not hinder him. Forgetful ourselves, help us to bear cheerfully the forgetfulness of others. Give us courage, and faith, and the quiet mind. Give life to our good intentions, lest they be still-born. Bless us in all that is right, and correct us in all that is wrong. We ask of Thee this help and mercy for Christ's sake. Amen.

FRIDAY, JANUARY 17, 1947

O LORD OUR GOD, we remember Thy promise that wheresoever two or three are gathered together in Thy name, there Thou art in the midst of them. We claim that promise this morning, and pray that each one of us may be aware of Thy presence, for Thou knowest our needs, and how inadequate we feel ourselves to be in the presence of world problems and the challenges of this hour. If Thou wilt help us, O Lord, then shall we be better than we are, wiser than we know, and stronger than we dream.

In this prayer, we bring unto Thee the members of this body, its officers and its servants, for Thy blessing; men who feel the weight of responsibility and the need of divine guidance; men who often are sorely tempted and who need the support of Thy grace. Bestow upon them the courage to do the right as Thou hast given them to see the right, and make it clear unto us all, for Jesus' sake. Amen.

MONDAY, JANUARY 20, 1947

"DEAR LORD and Father of mankind,
    Forgive our feverish ways;
Reclothe us in our rightful mind,
In purer lives Thy service find,

6

In deeper reverence, praise,
"Take from our souls the strain and stress,
And let our ordered lives confess
The beauty of Thy peace."

Deliver us, O Lord, from the foolishness of impatience. Let us not be in such a hurry as to run on without Thee. We know that it takes a lifetime to make a tree; we know that fruit does not ripen in an afternoon, and Thou Thyself didst take a week to make the universe.

May we remember that it takes time to build the nation that can truly be called God's own country. It takes time to work out the kind of peace that will endure. It takes time to find out what we should do; what is right, and what is best.

Slow us down, O Lord, that we may take time to think, time to pray, and time to find out Thy will. Then give us the sense and the courage to do it, for the good of our country and the glory of Thy name. Amen.

WEDNESDAY, JANUARY 22, 1947

O FATHER IN HEAVEN, ere we become involved in the routine of the day, we pause to seek Thy help. Experienced in the ways of men, we know all too little of the ways of God. But Thou knowest us, each one of us, by name and by our needs. Turn our wayward minds and hearts to Thee. Forgive the faults and failures of the past and set us free from them. Forgive, O Lord, our failure to apply to ourselves the standards of conduct we demand of others. Forgive our slowness to see the good in our fellows and to see the evil in ourselves. In our differences may we be kind; in our agreements may we be humble, that Thy will may be

7

done in us, and through us in our beloved land. For Jesus' sake. Amen.

FRIDAY, JANUARY 24, 1947

O LORD OUR GOD, before whom all our pretenses fall away, who knowest our secret thoughts and our hidden fears, bless us this day with Thy Spirit and help us to discharge our duties faithfully and well. Ever sensitive to the hurting of our own feelings, may we be sensitive also to our grieving of Thy Holy Spirit when we give ourselves to the lesser loyalties and spend our time and our energies in that which is less than the highest and the best.

We pray for the President of the United States, the members of the Cabinet, the representatives of the people, the judges of the land, and all those in authority, that it may please Thee so to rule their hearts that they may rightly use the trust committed to them for the good of all people.

Raise up among us, we pray Thee, fearless men who know that only in the doing of Thy will can we find our peace. So make it plain to us this day, and give us the courage to do it. All this we beg for Jesus Christ's sake. Amen.

MONDAY, JANUARY 27, 1947

O GOD OF TRUTH, who alone canst lead men into the truth that is freedom and joy, be Thou our teacher as we seek to find the way of life in times that bewilder and challenge. Teach us better to know ourselves, that, knowing our weaknesses, we may be on guard. Teach us better to understand other people, that we may view their shortcomings with charity, their virtues with appreciation, and their kindness to us with gratitude.

Be with Thy servants in this place, in all things great and

small, so that small things become great and great things become possible. Father of mercies, bless their loved ones and their families and make their homes sanctuaries of love and peace where they may find spiritual resources for the strain and pressure of their duties here.

Give us now Thy spirit, to guide and direct our thinking, that when the day's work is over we may merit Thy "Well done." Through Jesus Christ our Lord. Amen.

WEDNESDAY, JANUARY 29, 1947

ALMIGHTY GOD, creator of all things, giver of every good and perfect gift, hear us this day as we seek Thy blessing upon our deliberations.

We acknowledge before Thee our shortcomings, our self-ishness, our smugness, and our pride. Forgive us wherein we have come short of Thy will for us and for our nation. Create within us clean hearts, and renew right spirits, that we may do better and be better. Forgive us our forgetfulness of the world's sore need and our contentment with things as they are.

Hear us when we pray for all those in places of influence and authority, that they may do right. Guide those who lead us; and touch Thy servants with Thy Holy Spirit, that their faith may be revived, their hope renewed, and their vision made clear and challenging. Give to them the conviction that with Thy help all things are possible—even the most difficult things that baffle us now. God forbid that any of us here should add to the problems of the hour, but rather resolve, by Thy help, to become part of the answer. So help us, God, for Jesus' sake. Amen.

FRIDAY, JANUARY 31, 1947

OUR FATHER, as we come before the Throne of Grace this day, we would not weary Thee with our constant begging. We would not be like petulant children, seeking diplomas without study, or wages without work. We thank Thee for lessons to learn and for work to do. May we apply ourselves to both. As Thy servants here sincerely seek to do right, make it plain to them. Knowing that criticism will come, help them to take from it what is helpful, and to forgive what is unjust and unkind. Amid all the pressures brought upon them, may they ever hear Thy still small voice, and follow Thy guidance for the good of all the people, that Thy will may be done in this nation, through these Thy servants. For Jesus' sake. Amen.

MONDAY, FEBRUARY 3, 1947

OUR FATHER, in the midst of the complicated situations of life and the unsolved problems of the world, deliver Thy servants from any sense of futility. Let them feel the support of the prayers of hosts of true patriots throughout this land and, above all, the uplift of everlasting arms. Cause them to understand that God's power has never been obstructed by difficulties, nor His love limited by the confusion of human plans. May the very failure of man's best resources impel us toward the resources of God. Cleanse our hearts of selfishness. Grant that all questions immediately before us may be made so plain that we shall have no forebodings as we make our decision, nor vain regrets after it is made. For Jesus' sake. Amen.

WEDNESDAY, FEBRUARY 5, 1947

FORGIVE US, O GOD, for all our boasting and our presumptuous sins of pride and arrogance, for these are days that humble us.

By Thy grace, we become more and more aware of our limitations and our weaknesses.

Let us not mistake humility for an inferiority complex, but help us to understand that with the proud and the self-sufficient Thou canst do nothing until Thou hast brought them to their knees.

We need Thy help, our Father, and we seek it humbly. We want to do right, and to be right; so start us in the right way, for Thou knowest that we are very hard to turn. Shed forth Thy grace upon us, O Lord, that each man here may say, "I can do all things through Christ which strengtheneth me." We ask it in His name. Amen.

FRIDAY, FEBRUARY 7, 1947

O LORD, teach us to number our days that we may apply our hearts to wisdom. Time is short, and no one of us knows how little time he has left. May we be found using wisely our time, our talents, and our strength. Break to us this day the "bread of life." Our hearts are hungry, as are the hearts of people everywhere. Save us from thinking, even for a moment, that we can feed our souls on things. Save us from the vain delusion that the piling up of wealth or comforts can satisfy. Save these, Thy servants, the chosen of the people, from the tyranny of the nonessential, from the weary round of that which saps strength, frays nerves, shortens life, and adds nothing to their usefulness to Thee and to this nation. Help them to give themselves to the important, and to recognize the trivial when they see it. Give them the courage to say "No" to everything that makes it more difficult to say "Yes" to Thee. For Jesus' sake. Amen.

WE THANK THEE, ALMIGHTY GOD, for the rich heritage of this good land; for the evidences of Thy favor in the past; and for the Hand that hath made and preserved us a nation. We thank Thee for the men and women who, by blood and sweat, by toil and tears, forged on the anvil of their own sacrifice all that we hold dear. May we never lightly esteem what they obtained at a great price. Grateful for rights and privileges, may we be conscious of duties and obligations.

On this day we thank Thee for the inspiration that breathes in the memory of Abraham Lincoln, and we pray that something of the spirit that was his may be ours today. Like him, may we be more concerned that we are on Thy side, than that Thou art on ours. In our hearts may there be, as there was in his, malice toward none and charity for all; that we may, together, with Thy blessing and help, "bind up the Nation's wounds, and do all which may achieve and cherish a just and lasting peace among ourselves and with all nations." Through Jesus Christ our Lord. Amen.

O THOU GREAT ARCHITECT of the Universe, whom, by the revelation of Thy Son our Lord, we may address as our Father, help us to understand what that means. As we are now united in our praying, so may we be united in our working, that, as a team, we may be doing together the will of our Father, who is not a God of any one party, of any one nation, or of any one race. Open our eyes that we may discern what God is doing, and our ears that we may hear what God is saying. And then, O God, give us all we need to take due notice and to govern ourselves accordingly. We ask these things in the strong name of Jesus Christ our Lord. Amen.

FRIDAY, FEBRUARY 14, 1947

O LORD OF OUR LIFE, we would know Thee better, that we might love Thee more, and thus be more useful to our fellow men. Make us hungry for Thy spirit and Thy power. Let Thy grace come upon us, that the will of our God may be known to us and done through us.

Let us not break faith with any of yesterday's promises, nor leave unrepaired any of yesterday's wrongs. Show us what we can do to make this world a better place for men to live in, that the down payment made by 300,000 of our men may not have been made in vain.

May the urgency of the world's need remind us that promises do not feed the hungry, nor resolutions give them shelter. May we be willing to act when Thou shalt show us what to do. We join our hearts in this prayer for Thy guidance. In the name of Jesus Christ our Lord. Amen.

MONDAY, FEBRUARY 17, 1947

OUR FATHER IN HEAVEN, we pray for the members of this body in their several responsibilities. Help them in their offices, in committees, and, above all, as they meet here in legislative session. May they never forget that what is said and done here is not done in a corner, but always under Thy scrutiny. May they feel the weight of their responsibility before Thee, and remember the influence of a good example, that all who come to this place may have a stronger faith in government of the people, by the people, for the people. May the senators so speak and act that all who wait upon them and serve them may be inspired, rather than disillusioned, by what they see and hear and are asked to do. Lord Jesus, make Thyself real to these men, that each may feel Thee sitting beside him, and hear Thy voice, and win Thine approval in all things. So help them, God, for Jesus' sake. Amen.

WEDNESDAY, FEBRUARY 19, 1947

WE RECOGNIZE, our Father, as George Washington saw so clearly, that "no people can be bound to acknowledge and adore the Invisible Hand which conducts the affairs of men than those of the United States. Every step by which they have advanced to the character of an independent nation seems to have been distinguished by some token of providential agency."

Believing that the Hand that hath brought us thus far will not forsake us now, but if we are willing will lead us on into further inspiration and service to all mankind, we would join our prayers this day with those of Christian women all over the world in this day of prayer. With so many souls united in intercession for our own beloved country and for all mankind, may there come an outpouring of Thy Spirit into our hearts and minds, that we shall feel it, and all men may know it.

"Lift us above unrighteous anger and mistrust, into faith and hope and charity, by a simple and steadfast reliance on Thy sure will."

We pray for some evidence in what is said and done here, that Thou hast been permitted a vote, and that men yielded to Thee. In Jesus' name. Amen.

FRIDAY, FEBRUARY 21, 1947

Our Father in Heaven, we know that Thou canst see the hidden things in every heart. If our intentions are good, help us to make them live in good deeds. If what we intend or desire makes us uncomfortable in Thy presence, take it from us, and give us the spirit we ought to have, that we may do what we ought to do. For Jesus' sake. Amen.

MONDAY, FEBRUARY 24, 1947

With all the resources of an infinite God available to them that ask Thee, forgive us, O Lord, for our lack of faith that begs for pennies when we could write checks for millions; that strikes a match when we could have the sun. Give to us the faith to believe that there is no problem before us that Thy wisdom cannot solve. As Thou hast guided men in the past, so guide these men today. At every desk may there be the whisper of Thy counsel. Help our leaders to weigh their words, that their words may carry weight, and, what is more, the echo of Thy will, for Jesus' sake. Amen.

WEDNESDAY, FEBRUARY 26, 1947

Give to us open minds, O God, minds ready to receive and to welcome such new light of knowledge as it is Thy will to reveal. Let not the past ever be so dear to change our minds, when that is needed. Let us be tolerant of the thoughts of others, for we never know in what voice Thou wilt speak.

Wilt Thou keep our ears open to Thy voice, and make us a little more deaf to whispers of men who would persuade us from our duty, for we know in our hearts that only in Thy will is our peace and the prosperity of our land. We pray in the lovely name of Jesus. Amen.

FRIDAY, FEBRUARY 28, 1947

LORD GOD OF HEAVEN, who hath so lavishly blessed this our beloved land, keep us humble. Forgive our boasting and our pride, and help us to share what Thou hast given. Impress us with a sense of responsibility, and remind us, lest we become filled with conceit, that one day a reckoning will be required of us.

Sanctify our love of country, that our boasting may be turned into humility and our pride into a ministry to all men everywhere. Make America Thy servant, Thy chosen channel of blessing to all lands, lest we be cast out, and our place be given to another. Make this God's own country by making us willing to live like God's people.

We ask these things in the name of Jesus Christ our Lord. Amen. MONDAY, MARCH 3, 1947

OUR FATHER, we know that we, by ourselves, are not sufficient for these days and for problems greater than the measure of our best wisdom. We pray that Thou wilt grant safe journey to our secretary of state as he carries the hopes and the prayers of this nation to the conference across the sea. A soldier himself, may he remember the price that was paid by millions for this opportunity, and may we, who pray for the success of the mission, be willing to pay the price for peace.

We believe, O Lord, that Thou wilt be present, with the marks of the nails in Thy hands, to lead them, and bless them, if they will receive Thy spirit.

May the ministers be aware of the Unseen Delegate. May Thy spirit move them, that there may be concession without coercion, and conciliation without compromise. May they, who represent us, represent Thee and, in Thy spirit, be courageous enough to begin anew, fearless enough to admit mistakes, and loving enough to forgive others. May we have the courage to apply what we applaud, to the end that we may help to establish Thy way of life for the people of the world. So may we all do the best we can, by Thy help, and be willing to leave the issue in Thy hands, through Jesus Christ our Lord. Amen.

WEDNESDAY, MARCH 5, 1947

O Thou Holy Spirit, who hast promised to lead us into all truth, prepare our hearts and minds for the business of this day, that we may behave with true courtesy and honor. Compel us to be just and honest in all our dealings. Let our motives be above suspicion. Let our word be our bond. Save us from the fallacy of depending upon our personality, or ingenuity, or position, to solve our problems. Since Thou hast the answers, make us willing to listen to Thee, that we may vote on God's side, and that God's will may be done in us. Through Jesus Christ our Lord. Amen.

FRIDAY, MARCH 7, 1947

17

Our Father, as we come into Thy presence this morning, we are saddened by the announcement of the great loss and bereavement sustained by one of the most distinguished members of this body. Our sympathy goes out to him, deep and tender, as we stand at his side sharing his sorrow as far as friends may and joining our prayers that he may feel even now the everlasting arms upholding him and Thy grace and Thy love sustaining him in this dark hour.

We give Thee thanks for his constant devotion, for the courage and the fidelity to duty that has marked these last years when he was called upon by Thy strange and mysterious providence to walk a hard road; and we give Thee thanks for the beauty and inspiration that his helpmeet provided in the difficult experiences they shared together.

We thank Thee for her charm and for the winsome beauty of her life and spirit, and we pray that Thy grace may be sufficient now for him who was her partner and for the members of the family who mourn her going.

We thank Thee for the hope Thou hast given us that there will come a day when the lost chords of life may be found again in that happy land, and all that is dark and mysterious now shall be revealed and its purposes made plain.

We pray that in this great sorrow, shared by each member of this body, we may be drawn closer to each other in true comradeship and fellowship. May sympathy unite our hearts to each other, and bind us to Thee, who dost mark our tears and hast promised to wipe them away.

So may Thy blessing be upon our brother now and upon all who are with him in the fraternity of sorrow, that their faith may be strengthened and their hope made bright and triumphant. Through Jesus Christ our Lord. Amen.

ALMIGHTY FATHER OF THE UNIVERSE, we come to Thee, conscious of our own shortcomings, but with the confidence and composure, knowing that having put our trust in Thee, our faith is well founded. May we tolerate nothing in our personal living which, if multiplied, would weaken our nation. Teach us that our country is no better than its citizens, and no stronger than those in whom it puts its trust. So may we see ourselves as Thou dost see us, that being ashamed we may seek forgiveness, and knowing our weaknesses may accept Thy strength. With Thy blessing upon us, we need not fear decisions, nor hesitate to act. So use us, guide us, and act through us, we ask in Jesus' name and for His sake. Amen.

GOD OF OUR FATHERS AND OUR GOD, in the gloom of this troubled hour, disclose the brightness of Thy presence and revive within us the hope of our faith. Deliver us from discouragement, and when we feel most helpless, make us turn to Thee for the answers Thou hast for every question. Enable us to see issues clearly, before crisis clouds them, and help us to choose the good course, lest relying upon our own wisdom we have to choose between evils.

Give us the boldness of a faith that has conviction as well as sentiment, and take from us all fear save that of failing to do Thy will.

We ask in the name of Him who died for all men, even Jesus Christ our Lord. Amen.

LORD JESUS, we turn in confidence unto Thee, since Thou wast tempted in all points like as we are, and yet without sin. Help us, that we may obtain victory over our temptations. We feel ashamed that we have so little power in our lives, and so often fall at the same old hurdles. Sometimes we grow discouraged and filled with doubts when we see so little evidence of growth in grace, in faith, and in spiritual perception.

We know that we are not what we ought to be; and we know that we are not yet what we will be; but we thank Thee that we are not what we once were. For whatever progress Thou hast made with us we give Thee thanks, and by Thy grace we are kept from despair. Help us to remember that they that wait upon the Lord shall renew their strength. May we wait and be made strong. Through Jesus Christ our Lord. Amen.

OUR FATHER IN HEAVEN, who dost know every secret of our hearts—all that we fear, all that we hope, and all of which we are ashamed—in this moment of confession, as each man looks into his own heart and mind, have mercy upon us all, and make us clean inside, that in all we do today we may behave with true courtesy and honor.

Compel us to be just and honest in all our dealings.

Let our motives be above suspicion.

Let our word be our bond.

Let us be kind in our criticism of others, and slow to judge, knowing that we ourselves must one day be judged.

We pray for a new spirit to come upon us that we may be able to do more and better work. Through Jesus Christ our Lord. Amen.   TUESDAY, MARCH 18, 1947

L ORD J ESUS, Thou who art the way, the truth, and the life, hear us as we pray for the truth that shall make men free. Teach us that liberty is not only to be loved, but also to be lived. Liberty is too precious a thing to be buried in books. It cost too much to be hoarded. Make us to see that our liberty is not the right to do as we please, but the opportunity to please to do what is right. So may America, through Thy servants, the members of this body, do what is right, that Thy blessing can rest upon their labors, and give them good conscience. Through Jesus Christ our Lord. Amen.

WEDNESDAY, MARCH 19, 1947

O L ORD OUR G OD, in the midst of the troubles that surround us, when compromises come home to roost and expediencies return to plague us, keep us from adding to the mistakes of the past. Save us from accepting a little of what we know to be wrong in order to get a little of what we imagine to be right. Help us to stand up for the inalienable rights of mankind and the principles of democratic government consistently and with courage, knowing that Thy power and Thy blessing will be upon us only when we are in the right. May we so speak, and vote, and live, as to merit Thy blessing. Through Jesus Christ our Lord. Amen.

THURSDAY, MARCH 21, 1947

LORD GOD OF HOSTS, Thou who art concerned about two billions of Thy creatures all over the earth, and yet who art concerned about each of us here as if we were an only child, Thou dost understand how hard it is for these Thy servants to keep in mind the millions of their fellow citizens for whom they must legislate. Thou knowest the clamor of voices in their ears, the constant tugging at their sleeves, forever trying to influence them; the small voices of the little men without money or names; the blatant voices of aggressive pressure groups; the big voices of selfish men and those working for personal gain, even the whispering inner voices of personal ambition, those insinuating voices holding out the lure of unmerited reward. Amid all the din of voices, give these Thy servants the willingness to take time to listen to Thy voice, knowing that if they follow the still small voice within, all Thy people will be served fairly, and all groups will get what they deserve. For Jesus' sake. Amen.

MONDAY, MARCH 24, 1947

OUR FATHER IN HEAVEN, as we pray for Thy guidance and help, we know that thou dost not intend prayer to be a substitute for work. We know that we are expected to do our part, for Thou hast made us, not puppets, but persons with minds to think and wills to resolve. Make us willing to think, and think hard, clearly, and honestly, guided by Thy voice within us, and in accordance with the light Thou hast given us. May we never fail to do the very best we can. We pray in the knowledge that it all depends on Thee. Help us then to work as if it all depended on us, that together we may do that which is pleasing in Thy sight. For Jesus' sake. Amen.

IN THE NAME OF JESUS CHRIST, who was never in a hurry, we pray, O God that Thou wilt slow us down, for we know that we live too fast. If we are to burn ourselves out, may it be in causes worth dying for. With all of eternity before us, make us take time to live— time to get acquainted with Thee, time to enjoy Thy blessings, and time to know each other. Deliver us from wasting time and teach us how to use it wisely and well.

We ask these things in the lovely name of Jesus. Amen.

OUR FATHER, that we stand to join our hearts in prayer is our acknowledgment of our great need of Thy guidance. We know that by ourselves we are not sufficient for these days, or for problems beyond the measure of our best wisdom. We are finding out that government of the people by the people is not good enough. We pray for government of the people by God. As this nation was founded under God, so we confess that our freedom, too, must be under God. Then, and only then, shall we achieve the peace we seek and the righteousness which alone exalteth a nation.

Hear our prayer, O God, and grant unto the members of this body Thy guidance, we humbly beseech Thee in Jesus' name. Amen.

LORD JESUS, who didst promise that by faith Thy disciples might remove mountains, increase our faith, till we no longer are awed by difficulties and frightened by problems. Hold us by Thy mighty hand until doubts shall cease and we begin to believe. Then shall we find all things possible, even Thy solutions to the questions that perplex us. For this we do pray. Amen.

FRIDAY, MARCH 28, 1947

OUR FATHER, as we seek Thy blessing, remind us that we cannot deceive Thee, though we may deceive ourselves. We dare not devise our own plans and draft our own schemes and then have the nerve to ask Thee to bless them, for we know that there are some things Thou wilt not and cannot bless. And unless Thy blessing accompanies what we do here, we waste our time. So guide us in what we propose, so that Thou canst bless us in what we produce. Through Jesus Christ our Lord. Amen.

MONDAY, MARCH 31, 1947

WHEN WE ARE honestly perplexed and have to do something, and are not sure what to do, we need Thy help, O God. In our choices let us not ask, "Will it work?" but, rather, "Is it right?" In this prayer we reach up to Thee. May we find that Thou art reaching down to us, and may we believe that when we are willing to listen Thou wilt speak. We wait upon Thee, O God. Through Jesus Christ our Lord. Amen.

TUESDAY, APRIL 1, 1947

O GOD, who didst love us all so much that Thou didst send us Jesus Christ for the illumination of our darkness and the salvation of our souls, give us wisdom to profit by the words He spoke, faith to accept the salvation He offers, and grace to follow in His steps.

As Christ said: "When ye stand praying, forgive, if ye have aught against any," O God, give us grace now so to do.

As Christ said: "It is more blessed to give than to receive," O God, give us grace today to think, not of what we can get, but of what we can give.

As Christ said: "Judge not, that ye be not judged," O God, give us grace this day first to cast out the beam out of our own eyes before we regard the mote that is in our brothers' eyes.

And when we find it hard to be humble, hard to forgive, O Lord, remind us how much harder it was to hang on the cross. Amen. WEDNESDAY, APRIL 2, 1947

GRACIOUS FATHER, we, Thy children, so often confused, live at cross-purposes in our central aims, and hence we are at cross-purposes with each other. Take us by the hand and help us to see things from Thy viewpoint, that we may see them as they really are. We come to choices and decisions with a prayer upon our lips, for our wisdom fails us. Give us Thine, that we may do Thy will. In Jesus' name. Amen.

THURSDAY, APRIL 3, 1947

WE KNOW, our Father, that there is a time to speak and a time to keep silence. Help us to tell the one from the other. When we should speak, give us the courage of our convictions. When we should keep silence, restrain us from speaking, lest, in our desire to appear wise, we give ourselves away. Teach us the sacraments of silence, that we may use them to know ourselves, and, above us, to know Thee. Then shall we be wise. Through Jesus Christ our Lord. Amen.   MONDAY, APRIL 7, 1947

ALMIGHTY AND ETERNAL GOD, Thou who alone knowest what lies before us this day, grant that in every hour of it we may stay close to Thee. Let us embark on no undertaking that is not in line with Thy will for us here, for our country and our world. Bestow Thy grace upon the presiding officer, the members, and the servants of this body. Illumine our minds and direct our thinking, that our thoughts and our actions may merit Thy blessing. For our Lord Christ's sake. Amen.

TUESDAY, APRIL 8, 1947

OUR FATHERS' GOD, to Thee, who art the author of our liberty, and under whom we have our freedom, we make our prayer. Make us ever mindful of the price that was paid to obtain that freedom and the cost that must be met to keep it. Help us in this nation so to live it that other men shall desire it and seek after it. Believing in it, give us the backbone to stand up for it. Loving it, may we be willing to defend it. In the strong name of Him who said, "If ye continue in My work, ye shall know the truth, and the truth shall make you free." Amen.

WEDNESDAY, APRIL 9, 1947

Our Father in heaven, we give Thee thanks for good weather and the lovely promises of spring. We thank Thee for good health, good friends, and all the things we so often take for granted. We thank Thee for the keen challenges of this hour, for work to do that demands the best we have and still finds us inadequate. Then may we seek Thy help, knowing that in partnership with Thee, in applying Thy will to our problems, there shall be no dull moments and no problems beyond solution. God bless us all and help us to be right and to do right. Through Jesus Christ our Lord. Amen.   THURSDAY, APRIL 10, 1947

We come in prayer to Thee, Lord Jesus, who never had to take back anything spoken, to correct anything said, or to apologize for any statement. Wilt Thou have pity upon our frailties and deliver us from pitying ourselves.

Bless the members of this body as they think together and work together in this Chamber, in committee rooms, and in their offices. Help them to stand up under the strains and the tensions of problems and decisions, of meetings and conferences, and the endless demands made upon them. Teach them how to relax and to make time to turn to Thee for guidance and for grace, and thus discover the secret of power. In Thy name we ask it. Amen.

FRIDAY, APRIL 11, 1947

O Lord our God, in the face of life's mysteries and its vast imponderables, give us faith to believe that Thou makest all things to work together for good to them that love Thee. Strengthen our conviction that Thy hand is upon us, to lead us and to use us in working out Thy purposes in the world. Even though we may not see the distant scene, let us be willing to take one step at a time and trust Thee for the rest. Amen.

WEDNESDAY, APRIL 16, 1947

O GOD OUR FATHER, in whom we trust, Thou alone dost know the end from the beginning, and we, Thy children, must needs walk by faith. We are anxious about the consequences of what we do. May that concern restrain us in our private lives as it does in our public duty. In our troubled minds there is confusion and honest perplexity. But we know there is no confusion with Thee. Wilt Thou guide us, that we may do what is right; and if we suffer for it, we shall be blessed.

This we ask in Christ's name, who was crucified, having done nothing amiss. Amen.

THURSDAY, APRIL 17, 1947

OUR FATHER, we yearn for a better understanding of spiritual things, that we may know surely what Thy will is for us and for our nation. Give to us clear vision that we may know where to stand and what to stand for— because unless we stand for something, we shall fall for anything.

Remind us, O God, that Thou hast not resigned. Harassed and troubled by the difficulties and uncertainties of the hour, we rest our minds on Thee, who dost not change. May it ever be in our minds as upon our coins that in God we trust. For Jesus' sake. Amen.

FRIDAY, APRIL 18, 1947

Lord Jesus, help us to see clearly that the pace at which we are living these days shuts Thee out of our minds and hearts, and leaves us, even with good intentions, to wander in the misty land of half-truth and compromise.

Deliver us, O God, from the God-helps-those-who-help-themselves philosophy, which is really a cloak for sheer unbelief in Thy ability and willingness to take care of us and our affairs.

Give to us a passion for that which is in principle excellent, rather than in politics expedient, for that which is morally right rather than socially correct.

These things we ask in Jesus' name. Amen.

MONDAY, APRIL 21, 1947

Lord Jesus, who didst fill three short years with the revelation of all eternity, in life, precept, and promise, that we have not yet learned and can never forget, help us to make every minute count, making time our servant and not our master. Thou didst never ask for time to prepare Thine answers, but always had the word of Truth for every occasion. Reveal to us now Thy word for today. Amen.

TUESDAY, APRIL 22, 1947

Our Father, help us to understand that when we try to live without Thee, we are unable to live with ourselves; and when we say "No" to Thee, we are denying our own best interest. Whatever other rewards or punishments Thou hast ordained, we are finding out that we cannot do wrong and feel right, for there is a law within Thy universe that acts around us and in us. Give to each one of us, we pray, that intelligent self-interest that shall persuade us to do Thy will. Teach us that obeying Thee and Thy will is a forced option—like eating. We do not have to eat, but if we do not, we cannot live. We are not forced to obey Thee, but if we do not, we hurt ourselves. Convict us of the folly of walking against Thy lights, that we may live longer and better.

By the grace and mercy of Jesus Christ our Lord. Amen.

WEDNESDAY, APRIL 23, 1947

Our Father, we in this place are weighed down by the problems of our nation and of our world. Convict us of our share of personal responsibility for the situation in which we find ourselves. May we confess our part in creating our dilemmas, lest we feel no obligation to solve them. Help us to quit waiting for the other fellow to change his attitude and his ways, lest we never give Thee the chance for which Thou hast been waiting to change us.

This we ask in the lovely name of Him who came to change us all, even Jesus Christ our Lord. Amen.

THURSDAY, APRIL 24, 1947

Our Father which art in heaven, we pray for all the people of our country, that they may learn to appreciate more the goodly heritage that is ours. We need to learn, in these challenging days, that to every right there is attached a duty and to every privilege an obligation. We believe that, in the eternal order of things, Thou hast so ordained it, and what Thou hast joined together let us not try to put asunder. Teach us what freedom is. May we all learn the lesson that it is not the right to do as we please, but the opportunity to please to do what is right. Above all, may we discover that wherever the Spirit of the Lord is there is freedom. May we have that freedom now, in His presence here, to lead us and to help us keep this nation free.

This we ask in Jesus' name. Amen.

FRIDAY, APRIL 25, 1947

WE UNITE OUR HEARTS, O God, in this prayer that Thou wilt teach us how to trust in Thee as a Heavenly Father who loves us and who is concerned about what we do and what we are. Forgive us that there are times when we find it hard, when it ought to be so easy. It is not that we have no faith, but that we seem so reluctant to put our faith in Thee. Men have proved to be untrustworthy, yet we trust each other. Banks have failed, still we write our checks. Depressions have upset our economy, still we carry on business in faith. Blizzards have made the winter drear, yet with the coming of spring we plant our seeds. Hurricanes have screamed across the land, yet we build our windmills. Give to us the faith to put our trust in Thee who dost hold in the hollow of Thy hand all things living. May we learn, before we blunder, that Thou art willing to lead us, to show us what to do, and that it is possible for us to know Thy will and to be partners with Thee in doing what is right.

This we ask in the name of Christ, who never made a mistake. Amen. MONDAY, APRIL 28, 1947

GIVE US OPEN EYES, our Father, to see the beauty all around us and to see in it Thy handiwork. Let all lovely things fill us with gladness and let them lift up our hearts in true worship.

Give us this day, O God, a strong and vivid sense that Thou art by our side. By Thy grace, let us go nowhere this day where Thou canst not come nor court any companionship that would rob us of Thine. Through Jesus Christ our Lord. Amen.

TUESDAY, APRIL 29, 1947

OUR FATHER IN HEAVEN, who dost love the whole world, save us from despair and fear as we ponder the little progress of the conference just concluded across the seas. Help us to see that there is gain in our statement of faith while others voice their fears, and that nothing is lost when our convictions and principles are expressed boldly and honestly in the midst of intrigue and suspicion. Keep us ever resolute in striving for the things for which so many of our men gave their lives in battle. Let us not throw away their sacrifice.

Since we seek unity and harmony in the world and in our own land, help us to achieve it in this place. If we, Thy servants, who pray together, who speak the same language, who share the same basic ideals, cannot work as a team, what hope have we that the leaders of other nations, with different languages, who do not pray together, whose ideals are so different, can achieve agreement? Help us, a hundred men, to find the secret of agreement, that we may show it to our own nation, and lead it into teamwork between management and labor, between every group and faction, that our nation may be one.

As we express our own ideas and listen to the ideas of those who differ with us, may we be humble enough to think about the third idea—Thine—and be persuaded by

Thy Holy Spirit to embrace it, and thus discover the secret of harmony.

In the name of Jesus Christ, who was always right. Amen.

Our Father, we would not weary Thee in always asking for something. This morning we would pray that Thou wouldst take something from us. Take out of our hearts any bitterness that lies there, any resentment that curdles and corrodes our peace. Take away the stubborn pride that keeps us from apology and confessing fault and makes us unwilling to open our hearts to one another. For if our hearts are closed to our colleagues, they are not open to Thee.

We ask Thy mercy in Jesus' name. Amen.

O Lord, Thou dost know the secrets that will remake Thy world, for Thou art the way. Help us to see that the forces that threaten the freedom for which we fought cannot be argued down, nor can they be shot down. They must be lived down. Give to the leaders of our nation the inspired ideas that shall lead this country into making the American dream come true.

Through Jesus Christ our Lord. Amen.

Most gracious God, facing the activities and the opportunities of another week, may we be eager and not reluctant. Keep us ever alert to the need for change, and open as channels for divine power. Help us to keep keen the

edges of our minds, to keep our thinking straight and true.
Give us the will to keep our passions in control and the
common sense to keep our bodies fit and healthy, that we
may be able to do what Thou hast called us to do.

Through Jesus Christ our Lord. Amen.

FORGIVE US, O God, that in this land so richly
blessed by Thee, we, Thy people, have been wasteful.
We have wasted the treasures of the earth, stolen the virtues
of the soil, in failing to restore after we had received. But
we have been wasteful of ourselves. We have wasted our
strength in enterprises not inspired of Thee. We have wasted
our talents in unworthy causes, wasted our love in loving the
unlovely. We have wasted our money for that which satisfieth
not. We have wasted our time in activities that profited
nothing. Forgive us all wherein we have been prodigal, and,
like the younger son, help us to come to ourselves, that we
may come to Thee, to be forgiven and restored.

This we ask in Jesus' name.

O GOD, our Father, who hast given us life and made
our earth so fair, reveal to us this day Thy heart of
infinite tenderness yearning for our love.

Make us to feel Thy spirit brooding over us, longing to
help us in our decisions, to save us from the pressures that
drive us and the tensions that break us down.

How strange it is, O lover of our souls, that Thou who art
love, who dost give love to hungry human hearts, shouldst
Thyself be the great unloved. Give us love to love Thee for

Thy love, and to love Him who first loved us and gave
Himself for us. Loving Thee, we shall love one another, and
loving one another, we shall do Thy will, and doing Thy
will, we shall always do right.

We make our prayer in the lovely name of Jesus. Amen.

WEDNESDAY, MAY 7, 1947

WE OPEN OUR HEARTS unto Thee, our Father,
and pray that Thy spirit may indwell each one of us
and give us poise and power. We believe in Thee, O God.
Give us the faith to believe what Thou has said. We trust in
Thee, O God. Give us the faith to trust Thee for guidance in
the decisions we have to make.

Help us to do our very best this day and be content with
today's troubles, so that we shall not borrow the troubles of
tomorrow. Save us from the sin of worrying, lest stomach
ulcers be the badge of our lack of faith. Amen.

THURSDAY, MAY 8, 1947

IN THIS, THE DAY that the Lord hath made, help
us, O God, to appreciate its beauty and to use aright its
opportunity.

Deliver us, we pray Thee, from the tyranny of trifles.
May we give our best thought and attention to what is
important, that we may accomplish something worthwhile.
Teach us how to listen to the prompting of Thy spirit, and
thus save us from floundering in indecision that wastes time,
subtracts from our peace, divides our efficiency, and
multiplies our troubles.

In the name of Jesus Christ our Lord. Amen.

MONDAY, MAY 12, 1947

FORBID IT, Lord, that we should walk through Thy beautiful world with unseeing eyes. Forgive us, our Father, for taking our good things for granted, so that we are in danger of losing the fine art of appreciation. With such dire need in every other part of the world, make us so grateful for the bounties we enjoy that we shall try, by Thy help, to deserve them more.

Where we are wrong, make us willing to change, and where we are right, make us easy to live with.

For Jesus' sake. Amen.

WEDNESDAY, MAY 14, 1947

LORD JESUS, when we get sick of ourselves, ashamed of our littleness, our selfishness, and petty things that irritate us, then let it be the beginning of spiritual health by making us willing to have Thee create in us clean hearts and renew right spirits within us. Hold us steady lest we lose our poise. Blunt our speech lest by cutting words and careless deeds we hurt our colleagues and the cause for which we speak. Where we differ in approaches to a problem, may we ever be open to consider another and a better way, guided, not by whether it be popular, or expedient, or practical, but always whether it be right.

Hear our prayer, O Lord, and help us, through Jesus Christ. Amen. FRIDAY, MAY 16, 1947

GOD OF OUR FATHERS, give unto us, Thy servants, a true appreciation of our heritage, of great men and great deeds in the past, but let us not be intimidated by feelings of our own inadequacy for this troubled hour.

Remind us that the God they worshipped and by whose help they laid the foundations of our nation is still able to help us uphold what they bequeathed and to give it new meanings. Remind us that we are not called to fill the places of those who have gone, but to fill our own places, to do the work Thou hast laid before us, to do the right as Thou hast given us to see the right, always to do the very best we can, and to leave the rest to Thee. Amen.

THURSDAY, MAY 22, 1947

O LORD OUR GOD, shed the light of Thy Holy Spirit within the minds and hearts of Thy servants in this place of responsibility and decision, that all who sincerely seek the truth may find it, and finding it may follow it, whatever the cost, knowing that it is the truth that makes men free. When we have the truth, let us not hit each other over the head with it, but rather use it as a lamp to lighten dark places, in order that we may see where we are going.

This we ask in the name of Jesus Christ our Lord. Amen.

FRIDAY, MAY 23, 1947

WE THANK THEE, our Father in Heaven, for this sacred moment when our hearts may be united in prayer, and when, forgetting all else save our need of Thy guidance and help, we may reach up to Thee as Thou art reaching down to us.

Let not the beauty of this day, or the glow of good health, or the present prosperity of our undertakings deceive us into a false reliance upon our own strength. Thou hast given us every good thing. Thou hast given us life itself with whatever talents we possess and the time and the opportunity to use them. May we use them wisely, lest they be curtailed or taken away.

Deliver us from the error of asking and expecting Thy blessing and Thy guidance in our public lives while closing the doors to Thee in our private living. Thou knowest what we are wherever we are. Help us to be the best we can be.

We ask in the name of Jesus Christ our Lord. Amen.

MONDAY, MAY 26, 1947

IF THOU, O LORD, shouldst mark iniquities, who among us could stand unafraid before Thee? For there is so much bad in the best of us, and so much good in the worst of us, that we dare not criticize each other. But Thou canst reprove us all.

Ere we begin our duties, cleanse Thou our minds and hearts. What no proper shame kept us from committing, let no false shame keep us from confessing. In this moment may we find grace to seek Thy pardon and find the joy of the Gospel of making a new beginning.

In the power of Christ our Lord and Master. Amen.

WEDNESDAY, MAY 28, 1947

ONCE AGAIN, our Father, the long weekend that brings rest and refreshment to so many of our people has brought disaster and sorrow to some, and our nation is sobered in the reflection that death is in the midst of life. Since we know not at what moment the slender thread may be broken for us, teach us to number our days that we may apply our hearts unto wisdom. And may we be compassionate, remembering the hearts that are sore and our brethren who languish in sorrow and affliction.

Take from us the selfishness that is unwilling to bear the burdens of others while expecting that others shall help us with ours. Make us so disgusted with our big professions and our little deeds, our fine words and our shabby thoughts, our friendly faces and our cold hearts, that we shall pray sincerely this morning for a new spirit and new attitudes. Then shall our prayers mean something, not alone to ourselves but to our nation.

In the name of Jesus Christ our Lord. Amen.

MONDAY, JUNE 2, 1947

WE PRAY, O God, that Thou wilt fill this sacred minute with meaning, and make it an oasis for the refreshment of our souls, a window cleaning for our vision, and a recharging of the batteries of our spirits. Let us have less talking and more thinking, less work and more worship, less pressure and more prayer. For if we are too busy to pray, we are far busier than we have any right to be.

Speak to us, O Lord, and make us listen to Thy broadcasting station that never goes off the air.

Through Thy Holy Spirit, who is waiting to lead us into truth. Amen.

TUESDAY, JUNE 3, 1947

O LORD OUR GOD, as we seek Thy guidance this day, we do not ask to see the distant scene, knowing that we can take only one step at a time. Make that first step plain to us, that we may see where our duty lies, but give us a push, that we may start in the right direction.

Through Jesus Christ our Lord. Amen.

WEDNESDAY, JUNE 4, 1947

39

Our Heavenly Father, if it be Thy will that America should assume world leadership, as history demands and the hopes of so many nations desire, make us good enough to undertake it.

We consider our resources in money and in men, yet forget the spiritual resources without which we dare not and cannot lead the world.

Forgive us all for our indifference to the means of grace Thou hast appointed. Thy Word, the best seller of all books, remains among us the great unread, the great unbelieved, the great ignored.

Turn our thoughts again to that Book which alone reveals what man is to believe concerning God and what duty God requires of man.

Thus informed, thus directed, we shall understand the spiritual laws by which alone peace can be secured, and learn what is the righteousness that alone exalteth a nation.

For the sake of the world's peace and our own salvation, we pray in the name of Christ Thy revelation. Amen.

THURSDAY, JUNE 5, 1947

O God, our Heavenly Father, restore our faith in the ultimate triumph of Thy plan for the world Thou hast made. In spite of present difficulties, our disappointments and our fears, reassure us that Thou art still in control. When we become frustrated and give up, remind us that Thou art still holding things together, waiting and working and watching. When we make mistakes, help us to remember that Thou dost not give up on us. Forbid it, Lord that we should give up on Thee and forget that all

things work together for good to them that love Thee.
Through Jesus Christ our Lord. Amen.

FRIDAY, JUNE 6, 1947

FORGIVE US, O God, that we are so anxious, in all we say and do, to have the approval of men, forgetting that it is Thy approval that brings us peace of mind and clear conscience. Make us aware of the record Thou art writing— the record that one day will be read by the Judge of all the universe. We need to remember that there is no party in integrity, no politics in goodness. We pray for Thy grace and Thy help to do better and to be better.
Through Jesus Christ. Amen.

MONDAY, JUNE 9, 1947

O LORD OF OUR LIVES, wilt Thou teach us true discrimination, that we may be able to discern the difference between faith and fatalism, between activity and accomplishment, between humility and an inferiority complex, between a passing salute to God and a real prayer that seeks to find out God's will. We can stand criticism. We can stand a certain amount of pressure. But we cannot stand, O God, the necessity of making grave decisions with nothing but our own poor human wisdom. Our heads are not enough and our hearts fail us. Cabbages have heads, but they have no souls. We, who are created in the image of God, are restless and unhappy until we know that we are doing Thy will by Thy help.
That is what we pray for, through Jesus Christ our Lord. Amen. TUESDAY, JUNE 10, 1947

Our Father in heaven, as we unite in prayer for Thy blessings upon the members of this body, we know that Thou art lovingly concerned about the way we live and how we wear ourselves out, taking less care of ourselves than we do of our cars. Bless Thy servants, the senators, with good health, and good sense to preserve it. Bless the members of their families. May they commit them all to Thy care, that no leaden anxiety shall keep any man from doing his best work. We feel that we have to do so many things that we would rather not do, as we plead that we have no time to do some things we know very well we should do. Help us to make wise choices and proper use of our time.

We wait upon Thee for the continual answer to our prayers.

In the name of Christ, Thy Son. Amen.

WEDNESDAY, JUNE 11, 1947

God of our fathers, in whose name this Republic was born, we pray that by Thy help we may be worthy to receive Thy blessings upon our labors.

In the trouble and uneasy travail before the birth of lasting peace, when men have made deceit a habit, lying an art, and cruelty a science, help us to show the moral superiority of the way of life we cherish. Here may men see truth upheld, honesty loved, and kindness practiced. In our dealing with each other, may we be gentle, understanding, and kind, with our tempers under control. In our dealings with other nations, may we be firm without obstinacy, generous without extravagance, and right without compromise. We do not pray that other nations may love us, but that they may know that we stand for what is right, unafraid, with the courage of our convictions.

May our private lives and our public actions be consistent with our prayers.

Through Jesus Christ our Lord. Amen.

WE CONFESS, our Father, that we know in our hearts how much we need Thee, yet our swelled heads and our stubborn wills keep us trying to do without Thee.

Forgive us for making so many mountains out of molehills and for exaggerating both our own importance and the problems that confront us.

Make us willing to let Thee show us what a difference Thou couldst make in our work, increasing our success and diminishing our failures. Give us the faith to believe that if we give Thee a hearing Thou wilt give us the answers we cannot find by ourselves.

In Jesus' name. Amen.

THOU MUST BE GRIEVED, O Lord, that, after nineteen hundred years, mankind never seems to learn how to live by faith, and still prefers worry to trust in God. We know what worry does to us, yet are all to reluctant to discover what faith could do. Since we strain at gnats and swallow camels, give us a new standard of values and the ability to know a trifle when we see it and to deal with it as such. Let us not waste the time Thou hast given us.

So help us God. Amen.

ONCE AGAIN, OUR FATHER, we come to Thee in prayer, on the same old terms, because of our need of Thy help and our faith that Thou dost govern in the affairs of men and wilt hear our prayer in the name of Christ Thy Son.

Thou hast given us the inner voice of conscience, and Thy Holy Spirit enables us to distinguish good from evil. But where we are to choose between two courses when both are good and commendable, then we need the crystal clarity of Thy guidance, that we may see one better than the other. Help us, O God, at the point of our uncertainty with Thee. Thou hast a plan. We would clasp Thy hand. That shall be unto us better than light and safer than a known way.

Through Jesus Christ our Lord. Amen.

WEDNESDAY, JUNE 18, 1947

OUR FATHER, when we become satisfied with ourselves, hold ever before us Thy demands for perfection.

Lest we become content with a good batting average, let us see the absolutes of honesty, of love, and of obedience to Thy will Thou dost require of us.

Seeing them, may we strive after them by Thy help.

Through Jesus Christ our Lord. Amen.

TUESDAY, JUNE 24, 1947

OUR FATHER, we are beginning to understand at last that the things that are wrong with our world are the sum total of all the things that are wrong with us as individuals. Thou has made us after Thine image, and our hearts can find no rest until they rest in Thee.

44

We are too Christian really to enjoy sinning and too fond of sinning really to enjoy Christianity. Most of us know perfectly well what we ought to do; our trouble is that we do not want to do it. Thy help is our only hope. Make us want to do what is right, and give us the ability to do it.

In the name of Christ the Lord. Amen.

THURSDAY, JUNE 26, 1947

TEACH US, O Lord, the disciplines of patience, for we find that to wait is often harder than to work.

When we wait upon Thee, we shall not be ashamed, but shall renew our strength.

May we be willing to stop our feverish activities and listen to what Thou hast to say, that our prayers shall not be the sending of night letters, but conversations with God.

This we ask in Jesus' name. Amen.

FRIDAY, JUNE 27, 1947

LORD JESUS, we know of no better way to begin the work of another week than by rededicating our lives to Thee, resolving to trust Thee and to obey Thee and to do our very best to serve Thee by serving our fellow men. In these days that call for understanding, for mercy, for the salvation of men's souls and the healing of their bodies, may we have Thy spirit that we may work to that end, for Thou art the Saviour of the world, and we have no hope apart from Thee.

Hear our prayer for Thy mercy's sake. Amen.

MONDAY, JUNE 30, 1947

TEACH US, our Father, how to look at the things
we see, and to look at them without bias or prejudice.
We may not know how much of our troubles are caused by
refusing to look at the facts or by viewing them so
differently.

We are all too familiar with "dirty looks," "scornful
looks," "unbelieving looks," "black looks." Give to us
discerning and understanding looks. With the truth
waiting to be looked at, discovered, and applied, forgive
us when we refuse to look at it or to welcome it. If Thou
wilt help us to cast the mote of prejudice and pride out of
our eyes, then shall we see clearly.

We pray for good sight and good sense, in the name of
Jesus Christ. Amen.

TUESDAY, JULY 1, 1947

LORD OF OUR LIVES, we pray that Thou wilt fill
with new meanings this sacred moment of prayer.
Help us to feel and to believe that we are talking with God.
In this interlude of intercession, may we forget all else save
our deep need of Thy guidance and Thy help. In our hearts
are fears and frustrations, and we cannot view the future of
our world without misgivings. If there is a way for this God-
believing nation to live at peace with nations that deny
Thee, Thou wilt have to reveal it to us, for we have not
found it yet.

The disappointments and indecisions in our own lives
teach us that we, ourselves, are not in tune with Thy will for
us. God help us, and save us, and tell us what to do.

May the Great Physician minister to our brethren in
sickness, and the sympathizing Jesus be near to those in

trouble, and the Holy Spirit be in our hearts and minds this day, we ask in Jesus' name. Amen.

WEDNESDAY, JULY 2, 1947

GOD OF OUR FATHERS, whose Almighty hand hath made and preserved our nation, grant that our people may understand what it is they celebrate tomorrow.

May they remember how bitterly our freedom was won, the down payment that was made for it, the installments that have been made since this republic was born, and the price that must yet be paid for our liberty.

May freedom be seen, not as the right to do as we please, but as the opportunity to please to do what is right.

May it ever be understood that our liberty is under God and can be found nowhere else.

May our faith be something that is not merely stamped upon our coins, but expressed in our lives.

Let us, as a nation, not be afraid of standing alone for the rights of men, since we were born that way, as the only nation on earth that came into being "for the glory of God and the advancement of the Christian faith."

We know that we shall be true to the Pilgrim dream when we are true to the God they worshiped.

To the extent that America honors Thee, wilt Thou bless America, and keep her true as Thou hast kept her free, and make her good as Thou hast made her rich. Amen.

THURSDAY, JULY 3, 1947

O GOD OUR FATHER, we pray for Thy wisdom and Thy guidance for the members of this body as they meet in this troubled hour to consider what this

47

nation should do about hunger that knows no politics and want that will not wait.

We cannot escape history: that we have found out. May we also discover that we cannot evade responsibility. By Thy Holy Spirit awaken the conscience of America, that our people may be willing to put humanity first.

Give to our leaders the highest motives, and the courage to propose that which will be worthy of Thy blessing, lest we do the right things for the wrong reasons.

Help our senators to see what Thy plan is, in the name of Jesus Christ, who, being rich, for our sakes became poor. Amen.   MONDAY, NOVEMBER 17, 1947

GOD OF OUR FATHERS AND OUR GOD, give us the faith to believe in the ultimate triumph of righteousness, no matter how dark and uncertain are the skies of today.

We pray for the bifocals of faith—that see the despair and the need of the hour, but also see, further on, the patience of our God working out His plan in the world He has made.

So help Thy servants to interpret for our time the meaning of the motto inscribed on our coins.

Make our faith honest by helping us this day to do one thing because Thou hast said, "Do it," or to abstain because Thou hast said, "Thou shalt not."

How can we say we believe in Thee, or even want to believe in Thee, when we do not anything Thou dost tell us?

May our faith be seen in our works. Through Jesus Christ our Lord. Amen.

MONDAY, NOVEMBER 24, 1947

48

O LORD, keep strong our faith in the efficacy of prayer as we unite our petitions in this sacred moment.

We have asked for Thy guidance in difficult decisions many times, yet it has not always come when we thought it should come.

Many of the situations and relationships which we have asked Thee to change have remained the same.

Forgive us for thinking, therefore, that Thou art unwilling to help us in our dilemmas, or that there is nothing Thou canst do.

Remind us, our Father, that when we plug in an electric iron and it fails to work, we do not conclude that electricity has lost its power, nor do we plead with the iron.

We look at once to the wiring to find what has broken or blocked connection with the source of power.

May we do the same with ourselves, that Thou mayest work through us to do Thy will.

This we ask in Jesus' name. Amen.

TUESDAY, NOVEMBER 25, 1947

OUR FATHER IN HEAVEN, if ever we had cause to offer unto Thee our fervent thanks, surely it is now, on the eve of our Thanksgiving Day, when we, the people of this nation, are comfortable, well-fed, well-clad, and blessed with good things beyond our deserving. May gratitude, the rarest of all virtues, be the spirit of our observance.

Let not feasting, football, and festivity end in forgetfulness of God.

May the desperate need of the rest of the world, and our own glorious heritage, remind us of the God who led our fathers every step of the way by which they advanced to the character of an independent nation.

May the faith and conviction of George Washington be renewed in us as we remember his words: ". . . there is no truth more thoroughly established that there exists in the economy and course of nature an indissoluble union between virtue and happiness; between duty and advantage; between the genuine maxims of an honest and magnani-mous policy and the solid rewards of public prosperity and felicity; since we ought to be no less persuaded that the propitious smiles of Heaven can never be expected on a nation that disregards the eternal rules of order and right which Heaven itself has ordained. . . ."

For if we do not have the grace to thank Thee for all that we have and enjoy, how can we have the effrontery to seek Thy further blessings?

God give us grateful hearts. For Jesus' sake. Amen.

WEDNESDAY, NOVEMBER 26, 1947

O LORD, lift from our hearts all the discouragement, the cynicism, and the distrust of one another that destroys our faith in the little people who make up this republic and eats at the very foundations of our democracy.

Give to our leaders faith in our way of life, so that, instead of indicting other philosophies, we shall inspire our own. Give them faith in the people, in their deep desire to do whatever is for the good of all, in their willingness to make personal sacrifices for a good cause.

May we have courageous leadership, based on faith and not on fear—leadership that goes out in front and is not forever running to catch up with a band wagon.

Lord, increase our faith, through Jesus Christ our Lord.
Amen.

❧ AS WE COME TOGETHER IN PRAYER, O God,
we know that there is nothing in our hearts, in our
minds, or in our past that we can hide from Thee, for our
lives are all of one piece in Thy sight—not partitioned as we
like to think.

Therefore deliver us from the error of seeking and
expecting Thy guidance in our public lives while we close
the door to Thee in our private living.

Help us to be good men, that we may become good
leaders. For this day, before we reach any decisions, make us
willing to ask, "What would Jesus do?"

Then give us courage and the grace so to act.

We ask it in His lovely name. Amen.

❧ THOU, O GOD, art our Father, and to our Father we
come in this prayer. Reassure us that we have, each one,
a place in Thy heart and are precious in Thy sight.

We know that we have offended Thee by some of the
things we have done. We know that Thou canst not bless all
that we undertake and dost not approve of all our attitudes.
But we would hold on to that love Thou hast for each one of
us—the love that wilt not let us go and wilt not let us off.

When we are overwhelmed by our sense of littleness in
the world, may we remember that Thou hast made us all
different, hast given to each of us life for a purpose, and if
we fail it will never be fulfilled.

As our Lord preached some of His greatest sermons to

audiences of one, may He now whisper to each one of us, as we wait upon Him, yielded and still. Amen.

MONDAY, DECEMBER 8, 1947

IT IS GOOD, O Lord, that it is not custom that brings us again into this sacred moment of prayer, but our deep sense of need.

Forgive us all that we talk too much and think too little. Forgive us all that we worry so often and pray so seldom. Most of all, O Lord forgive us that, so helpless without Thee, we are yet so unwilling to seek Thy help.

Give us grace to seek Thee with the whole heart, that seeking Thee we may find Thee, and finding Thee may love Thee, and loving Thee may keep Thy commandments and do Thy will. Through Jesus Christ our Lord. Amen.

WEDNESDAY, DECEMBER 10, 1947

OUR FATHER IN HEAVEN, be gracious unto Thy servants, the senators of the United States. Give them strength for the tasks of this day and guide them in their labors. When they are tempted to wonder if a righteous peace is not an impossible dream, remind them that Thou are not senile, or asleep, or defeated. A different world cannot be built by indifferent people. Let us never give up hope of the possibility of change.

When we feel the pressure of crisis, remind us that Thou hast plenty of time. We have to remember that Thou art never in a hurry and wilt not be rushed by the deadlines of impatient men or by the violence of the wicked. Give us the grace to wait upon Thee, for they that wait upon the Lord shall renew their strength. They shall mount up with wings as the eagles. They shall run and not be weary. They shall walk and faint not.

Grant these mercies unto Thy servants, through Jesus Christ our Lord. Amen.　　FRIDAY, DECEMBER 12, 1947

OUR FATHER, as our heads are bowed in prayer, may our hearts be open to Thy Spirit, lest we say words with our hearts not in them, and make Thee yawn at the emptiness of our petition, or make Thee angry at the insincerity of what we do.

Give us faith to believe in prayer, and in Thy willingness to work in us that Thy will may be done among the nations and in our own land. We ask this in Jesus' name. Amen.
　　　　　　　　MONDAY, DECEMBER 15, 1947

LORD JESUS, in the hush of this moment, we pray that Thy tender Spirit may steal into our hearts and reveal to us how near and how dear Thou art.

There are times when Thou art not real to us, and we know why. It is not because Thou hast withdrawn from us, but because we have wandered away from Thee; not because Thou art not speaking, but because we are not listening; not because Thy love for us has cooled, but because we have fallen in love with things instead of persons.

O Lord, melt the coldness of our hearts that we may again fall in love with Thee who didst love us. Amen.
　　　　　　　TUESDAY, DECEMBER 16, 1947

LET US NOW REJOICE, most gracious God, in the love Thou hast shown toward us, opening up to us a way

whereby we might be delivered from our sin and foolishness.
We have found out that we cannot do wrong and feel right. By
our tolerance of some wrongs, we have come close to being
intolerant of the right. Make us bold enough to confront the
face of evil and of wrong, even when it bears our own image.
May we see that in every choice we make we are for Thee or
against Thee. God, help us to keep our moral voting record
straight. Through Jesus Christ our Lord. Amen.

WEDNESDAY, DECEMBER 17, 1947

OUR FATHER, let not my unworthiness stand
between Thee and the members of this body as we
join in prayer.

Hear not the voice that speaks, but listen to the yearnings
of the hearts now open before Thee in this moment when
each one of us is alone with Thee.

May the love of God, which is broader than the measure
of man's mind; the grace of our Lord Jesus Christ, which is
sufficient for all our need; and the fellowship of the Holy
Spirit, who shall lead us into all truth, be with us all this day.
Amen.   THURSDAY, DECEMBER, 18, 1947

WE THANK THEE, O God, for the return of the
wondrous spell of this Christmas season that brings its
own sweet joy into our jaded and troubled hearts.

Forbid it, Lord, that we should celebrate without
understanding what we celebrate, or, like our counterparts
so long ago, fail to see the star or to hear the song of glorious
promise.

As our hearts yield to the spirits of Christmas, may we
discover that it is Thy Holy Spirit who comes—not a

sentiment, but a power—to remind us of the only way by which there may be peace on the earth and good will among men.

May we not spend Christmas, but keep it, that we may be kept in its hope, through Him who emptied Himself in coming to us that we might be filled with peace and joy in returning to God. Amen.

FRIDAY, DECEMBER 19, 1947

EIGHTIETH CONGRESS
SECOND SESSION

OUR FATHER, who art Lord of heaven and of all earth, Thou knowest the difficulties these men have to face and the grave decisions they must make.

Have mercy upon them, for Jesus' sake. Amen.

TUESDAY, JANUARY 6, 1948

O Saviour of the world, Thou who hast a plan for peace and a program for all the nations, make it plain, and make us see it clearly, that we may find that which will work and will have Thy blessing.

Save us from hotheads that would lead us to act foolishly, and from cold feet that would keep us from acting at all.

May Thy Holy Spirit work among us to lead us into all truth. Through Jesus Christ our Lord. Amen.

WEDNESDAY, JANUARY 7, 1948

LORD, Thou wilt still be here after this prayer is said, and we would have it so, for we know deep down in our hearts that without Thy help we can do nothing abiding.

Without Thee we shall discuss more and more and settle less and less.

Unite, we pray Thee, the leaders of our nation behind the right way to achieve a just and lasting peace in our land and in all the world, that we may win it together, lest we lose it apart. Amen. FRIDAY, JANUARY 9, 1948

57

LORD JESUS, we need Thy power, obtained through prayer, to solve problems, decide issues, and to do Thy will. But let us not imagine that this formal prayer can take the place of private petition. May there arise from every desk the silent prayer that seeks to know Thy will. We long for such guidance that when a thing is right, we shall all know it; and when it is wrong, it will not be proposed. We would not run away from truth, but find a refuge in it. We would not avoid the discipline of hard thinking, but deliver us O Lord, from wrong thinking that leads to wrong conclusions. Guide us this day, for Thy mercy's sake. Amen.

MONDAY, JANUARY 12, 1948

WE ARE GLAD, Our Father, that troubles are cannibals—the big ones eat up the little ones.

But may it not be so with our duties and responsibilities. Help our senators to keep a sane perspective, lest the big issues overshadow the lesser ones, and they fail to do Thy will with them. In all things, big and little, reveal to us Thy wisdom and Thy love.

Through Jesus Christ our Lord. Amen.

WEDNESDAY, JANUARY 14, 1948

OUR FATHER, we turn to Thee because we are sore vexed with our own thoughts. Our minds plague us with questionings we cannot answer, and history confronts us with responsibilities we cannot evade. Who among us is sufficient for these things?

We are humbled by our experience of failure and driven by pressure to act before we are sure what Thou wouldst have us do. Thou knowest our deadlines as Thou knowest

58

our need. We cannot push Thee, for Thou wilt not be hurried. But only Thou canst keep us from being pushed.

Give us, therefore, the unhurried mind and the untroubled heart, by the mercies of Christ our Lord. Amen.

FRIDAY, JANUARY 16, 1948

O GOD, we turn to Thee in the faith that Thou dost understand and art very merciful.

Some of us are not sure concerning Thee; not sure how Thou dost reveal Thy will to us; not sure that it is possible for us to know, in every decision, just what Thou desireth Thy servants to do. But if we could say, "This is what God wants us to do," none would vote against it, and how much time and temper and money would be saved.

Make each one of us willing to yield himself to Thee in prayer and obedience.

Come and deliver us, O Holy Spirit, for we have no hope in ourselves. Amen.   MONDAY, JANUARY 19, 1948

O LORD MOST HIGH and very near, to whose mind the past and the future meet in this very day, hear us as we pray.

The great questions that stand unanswered before us defy our best wisdom.

Though our ignorance is great, at least we know we do not know.

When we do not know what to say, keep us quiet.

When we do not know what to do, let us ask of Thee, that we may find out.

We dare to ask for light upon only one step at a time.

We would rather walk with Thee than jump by ourselves.

We ask this in the name of Jesus Christ, who promised to send us a guide into all truth. Amen.

WEDNESDAY, JANUARY 21, 1948

O GOD OUR FATHER, we pray that the people of America, who have made such progress in material things, may now seek to grow in spiritual understanding.

For we have improved means, but not improved ends. We have better ways of getting there, but we have no better places to go. We can save more time, but are not making any better use of the time we save.

We need Thy help to do something about the world's true problems—the problem of lying, which is called propaganda; the problem of selfishness, which is called self-interest; the problem of greed, which is often called profit; the problem of lust, masquerading as love; the problem of materialism, the hook which is baited with security.

Hear our prayers, O Lord, for the spiritual understanding which is better than political wisdom, that we may see our problems for what they are. This we ask in Jesus' name. Amen.

MONDAY, JANUARY 26, 1948

OUR FATHER, it seems hard to care for those we find it far easier to hate, to love those whom we regard as unlovely, to spend our lives for those who are so ungrateful.

If we are to learn, Thou must be our teacher.

Since we will be criticized, let it be for doing too much or too little, rather than for doing nothing.

Teach us to trust not to cleverness or learning, but to that inward faith which can never be denied.

Lead us out of confusion to simplicity. In the name of
Jesus Christ. Amen.

WEDNESDAY, JANUARY 28, 1948

O LORD OUR GOD, even at this moment as we
come blundering into Thy presence in prayer, we are
haunted by memories of duties unperformed, promptings
disobeyed, and beckonings ignored.

Opportunities to be kind knocked on the door of our
hearts and went weeping away.

We are ashamed, O Lord, and tired of failure.

If Thou art drawing close to us now, come nearer still, till
selfishness is burned out within us and our wills lose all their
weakness in union with Thine own. Amen.

FRIDAY, JANUARY 30, 1948

LORD, we are finding that without Thee we can do
nothing. Let not foolish pride or stubborn will keep us
from confessing it.

Help us, O Lord, when we want to do the right thing, but
know not what it is. But help us most when we know
perfectly well what we ought to do and do not want to do it.

Have mercy upon us, Lord, and help us for Jesus' sake.
Amen. MONDAY, FEBRUARY 2, 1948

WE CONFESS, O Lord, that we think too much of
ourselves, for ourselves, and about ourselves.

If our Lord had thought about Himself, we would not
now be bowed in prayer, nor have the liberty in which and
for which we pray.

If the great men whom we honor for their part in building our nation had thought about themselves, we would have no free republic today. Help us to see, O Lord, that "I" is in the middle of sin, and let no man among us think more highly of himself than he ought to think, to the end that we may be used of Thee in Thy service for the good of all mankind.

Through Jesus Christ our Lord. Amen.

THURSDAY, FEBRUARY 5, 1948

MOST MERCIFUL FATHER, strengthen our faith, we pray, and save us from discouragement. Let not our hearts fail us when, after a war to set peoples free, there is less freedom in the world than there was before. Setting up standards of right and justice, we have seen them betrayed for money and mocked by selfishness. We have tried to forgive our enemies, we have humbled ourselves before haughty and cruel men, but we have not changed their hearts. Only Thou canst do that. But it takes faith to wait.

So we are tempted to despair of our world. Remind us, O Lord, that Thou hast been facing the same thing in all the world since time began.

But let not our hearts become hard or our spirits bitter. Keep our souls in faith and in hope. Through Jesus Christ our Lord. Amen.

MONDAY, FEBRUARY 9, 1948

OUR FATHER, as we remember the great men who by their trust in Thee helped to give this nation its glorious heritage, remind us that we honor them best when we follow their good example.

Give to the people of America, and to their leaders, the

old-fashioned honesty, and the old-fashioned love of country that sought to give rather than to get.

Help us to acknowledge our dependence upon the patience that forgives our failures, the truth that indicts our compromise and our hypocrisy.

We ask Thee not for tasks more suited to our strength, but for strength more suited to our tasks.

May we so live that the sacrifices that have been made for our liberty shall not have been in vain.

This we ask in the name of Thy dear Son, our Lord and Master, Jesus Christ. Amen.

WEDNESDAY, FEBRUARY 11, 1948

Our Father, on this World Day of Prayer, we join the ten million women in our own country and their sisters in many other lands in this their petition for Christian fellowship and world brotherhood.

"Father of all mankind, we come in deep humility, giving Thee our thanks and praise.

"Here and now we confess our sins.

"Forgive us our mistakes and transgressions.

"Grant us faith to look with fearless eyes beyond the chaos of our world and time, knowing that out of this shall rise, lifted by Thy grace, peace with justice and a time of brotherhood.

"Vouchsafe unto us the will to work together.

"Create within us the unselfish purpose of Thy Son, who gave His life for all peoples, and may our deeds reflect the mind of Christ.

"Remove from us greed and suspicion.

"Lift us above pettiness and destroy the hate that is the

great destroyer. Throughout the earth, may that which we profess come alive in human relations.

"May we serve Thee better and love Thee more, that Thy kingdom may come on earth as it is in heaven. Through Jesus Christ Thy Son, our Lord." Amen.

FRIDAY, FEBRUARY 13, 1948

Our Heavenly Father, save us from a worship of the lips while our hearts are far away.

In the battle now being fought in the realm of ideas, where deadly attacks are made upon our greatest treasure, our belief in God and the Gospel of Christ, deliver us from the peril of indifference, for we know that rust will crumble a metal when hammer blows will only harden it.

May this minute of prayer find each one of us, in his own way, reaching out for Thy help and guidance.

Hear our prayers and be with us this day. We ask in Jesus' name. Amen.

TUESDAY, FEBRUARY 17, 1948

O God, be merciful when we pray with half our heart or listen with half our mind, and pity us that we are torn as we are and bedeviled with compromises.

Vainly we long for life without such difficult decisions, yet we know that we have only ourselves to blame for the tensions in which we live.

We need to pray that our own eyes be opened to the truth. Deliver us from the reservations that would pray: "Thy kingdom come—but not yet; Thy will be done on earth—by other people." Help each one of us to see that if Thy Holy Spirit is to lead America, He must be permitted to lead us.

If Thy will is to be done, we must do it.

O God, most merciful, consider not our cowardice, but forgive our failings.

Harken to those prayers of our hearts which come to us in high moments when we forget ourselves and think of Thee. Amen.

FRIDAY, FEBRUARY 20, 1948

O GOD, forgive the poverty and the pettiness of our prayers. Listen not to our words but to the yearnings of our hearts. Hear beneath our petitions the crying of our need.

Thou gavest men life and at the same time gavest them liberty, and Thou must help us who love liberty to keep it in these days when it is stolen and destroyed.

Help us to see that when other men lose their freedom our own freedom is threatened.

And may we meet the threats of this hour with courage and with boldness. Through Him whose truth makes us free indeed. Amen.

TUESDAY, MARCH 2, 1948

GRANT, O LORD, that this assembly of freemen, chosen to lead a nation that loves and lives its freedom, may give hope and help to all those who, loving liberty, long to live in it.

May no cowardice or callous selfishness make us reluctant to assume the responsibilities of leadership in a world hungry for hope.

This we ask in the name of Jesus Christ, who is the hope of our salvation. Amen.

FRIDAY, MARCH 5, 1948

ETERNAL GOD and our loving Father, we come to Thee this day in the name of Jesus Christ, who is the lover of our souls and the Saviour of all mankind.

May we feel His love and respond to it.

May His Spirit shine into lives that are darkened by worry, doubt, or fear.

Strengthen and guide all those who are sincerely trying to do what is right, and make it plain.

Make us more mindful of the needs of our fellow men and less absorbed in selfish concerns, that Christ may approve and bless what we do here this day.

We ask these things in His name. Amen.

MONDAY, MARCH 8, 1948

HEAVENLY FATHER to whom all mankind is dear, if we feel frustrated in efforts to achieve a just and lasting peace, how must Thou feel that men so long and so willfully refuse to heed Thy laws and live in Thy love.

We have found that peace does not come when guns are silenced, for the war is not really ended.

The job is not done when the fire engines drive away.

So deliver us from the blasphemy of optimism that is mere wishful thinking.

Save us from the delusion of health that we may find the cure for our sickness.

Teach us, O God, that what is needed is not new things, but new spirits.

Give us the uplifted face and the flashing eye that express a purpose in life that will make sacrifice a joy and discipline peace.

Through Jesus Christ our Lord. Amen.

TUESDAY, MARCH 9, 1948

66

O GOD OUR FATHER, let us not be content to wait and see what will happen, but give us the determination to make the right things happen.

While time is running out, save us from patience which is akin to cowardice.

Give us the courage to be either hot or cold, to stand for something, lest we fall for anything.

In Jesus' name. Amen.

WEDNESDAY, MARCH 10, 1948

O CHRIST, who givest peace to every believing heart, bestow that gift upon us now, for we are troubled and uneasy. Events in our world take away our hope and shatter our peace. We need to be reassured that peace is still possible and that God's will shall yet be done upon the earth.

We believe that God's judgments are sure and altogether right, but we do wonder how long Thou wilt suffer godless men to defy Thee and to destroy the dreams Thou hast planted in human hearts. May we trust, not in bombs, however powerful, but in Thee, in Thy might, in Thy love, and in Thy plan, and in our secret weapon, the prayers of them that love Thee. Through Jesus Christ our Lord. Amen.

THURSDAY, MARCH 11, 1948

OUR FATHER, when we long for life without trials and work without difficulties, remind us that oaks grow strong in contrary winds and diamonds are made under pressure. With stout hearts may we see in every calamity an opportunity, and not give way to the pessimism that sees in every opportunity a calamity.

Knowing that Thou art still upon the throne, let us get on with the job on hand, doing the best we can and leaving the rest to Thee. Help us to show ourselves to be good workmen who need not to be ashamed, rightly dividing the word of truth.

This we ask in Jesus' name. Amen.

FRIDAY, MARCH 12, 1948

O LORD, direct our hearts into the patience of Christ. Make strong our faith that God's will, though it may be hindered a time and obstructed by human blindness and folly and sin, must in the end be triumphant.

May all that we do be in accordance with the victory of God. Graciously minister to Thy servants, the members of this body, according to their needs.

Through Jesus Christ our Lord. Amen.

SATURDAY, MARCH 13, 1948

O SPIRIT OF THE LIVING GOD, breathe upon this assembled company Thy gracious power. As the coming of spring rouses Nature from winter sleep, so may Thy Spirit revive us, giving us new hope and a livelier faith. If we have never before been conscious of our need, make our souls hungry for Thee, O God, that we may no longer be content to be half alive, which is half dead. Give us fullness of life, set free from fear and doubt, that we may find new joy in our labors.

Through Jesus Christ our Lord. Amen.

MONDAY, MARCH 15, 1948

WE PRAY UNTO THEE, O God, and call Thee our Father. Since Thou art our Father, we are Thy children; and if Thy children, we need never despair, no matter how dark and troubled our horizons.

Teach us not to despise the life we are called to live, since it was given to us by Thee. Teach us not to neglect the task of today because we cannot see its eternal effect. Teach us not to neglect the little duties which are training us for a great stewardship.

Help us to give a good account of this day for Jesus' sake. Amen.   TUESDAY, MARCH 16, 1948

WE PRAY, O GOD, in this uncertain hour, that Thou wilt reveal Thyself and Thy will to the leaders of our nation.

Help them to see the right way to preserve the things so dearly bought and to resolve the difficulties that seem so great.

Inspire their thoughts by the mind of Christ coming into their minds and the courage to challenge America to accept the moral responsibilities of the spiritual leadership of the world.

May we not be afraid to face facts, however unpleasant. Take away the acrophobia of our souls that we may breathe the pure air of high ideals and lofty purpose without becoming light-hearted.

For the sake of the world, for the sake of peace, for the sake of America, for conscience' sake, help us to do the right thing. Amen.   WEDNESDAY, MARCH 17, 1948

OUR FATHER IN HEAVEN, save us from the conceit which refuses to believe that God knows more about government than we do, and deliver us from the stubbornness that will not seek God's help.

Today we claim Thy promise: "If any man lack wisdom, let him ask God, who giveth to all men liberally . . . and it shall be given him." Thou knowest, Lord, how much we need it. Make us willing to ask for it and eager to have it. In Jesus' name we pray. Amen.

THURSDAY, MARCH 18, 1948

O GOD OUR FATHER, as a battery is recharged without sound or motion, so wilt Thou, in this moment so precious, send Thy spirit into the hearts and minds of Thy servants, the senators of the United States.

With newness of life, with spiritual power, vision, and lively faith, enable them to meet all the demands of this day with glad anticipation, and give them peace. Through Jesus Christ our Lord. Amen.

FRIDAY, MARCH 19, 1948

OUR FATHER, give us the faith to believe that it is possible for us to live victoriously even in the midst of dangerous opportunity that we call crisis. Help us to see that there is something better than patient endurance or keeping a stiff upper lip and that whistling in the dark is not really bravery.

Trusting in Thee, may we have the faith that goes singing in the rain, knowing that all things work together for good to them that love Thee. Through Jesus Christ our Lord. Amen.

MONDAY, MARCH 22, 1948

LORD JESUS, in the days of this holy week of solemn remembrance, bring to our minds again Thy new commandment that we love one another.

With loving concerns in our hearts, may we cherish each other and be willing to put the welfare of others ahead of our own. In loving other people we shall best express our love for Thee. So help us to love that we may be loved for Thy name's sake. Amen.

TUESDAY, MARCH 23, 1948

GOD OF MERCY AND COMPASSION, Thou knowest our nature and readest our secret thoughts, and we can hide nothing from Thee.

Help us, then, to lay aside every disguise we wear before the face of man and find rest and peace in being what we are and nothing more. Enable us to put off all shame and pretense, so that from now on we may live a life of freedom and sincerity.

It is not dangerous to be honest, but help each one of us to be true to himself at his best, and make us the best we can be for the sake of Him who died for us all. Amen.

WEDNESDAY, MARCH 24, 1948

LORD JESUS, Saviour of the world, in Thy holy name we join our hearts in prayer.

This week, as we remember all Thou didst for us, we may be sure Thou hast not forgotten. For we will not let Thee forget.

With every sin of ours, we renew the pain Thy heart did know.

Every time we ignore Thee, forget Thee, and heed not

Thy way, we revive for Thee the loneliness Thou didst feel and the spiritual blindness that broke Thy heart.

O Lord, give us Thy grace that we may not crucify Thee afresh, but, loving Thee, keep Thy commandments.

With steady faith that Thy kingdom will yet be established upon the earth, help us to hasten its coming by letting Thee work in us and through us to do Thy will. Amen.

THURSDAY, MARCH 25, 1948

OUR HEARTS STILL SINGING with the beauty and joy of Easter, we pray to Thee, O Christ, to keep us under the spell of immortality.

May we never again think and act as if Thou wert dead. Let us more and more come to know Thee as a living Lord who hath promised to them that believe: "Because I live, ye shall live also."

Help us to remember that we are praying to the Conqueror of Death, that we may no longer be afraid nor be dismayed by the world's problems and threats, since Thou hast overcome the world.

In Thy strong name, we ask for Thy living presence and Thy victorious power. Amen.   MONDAY, MARCH 29, 1948

HEAR, O GOD, our Father, the earnest supplications of the senators gathered for this sacred moment of prayer and deepen our feelings of unity and fellowship as we pray with them and for them.

Give us wisdom to see that no good life comes without right discipline.

Give us the grace to impose it upon ourselves, lest others do it for us.

72

Help us to discipline our speech, that we may seek clarity rather than cleverness and sincerity instead of sarcasm.

Help us to discipline our thinking and our action, that in this place the world may see democracy at its best and us at our best for democracy and for Thee to use us.

In the name of Jesus Christ, Thy Son, our Lord. Amen.

THURSDAY, APRIL 1, 1948

Our Father, let us never be ashamed to come to Thee in prayer, for we are Thy children, Thou art our Father.

Together we pray for the members of this body who need the healing ministry of the Great Physician and for their loved ones concerning whom they are anxious.

O Christ, our Saviour, Thou art still the sympathizing Jesus. Be near this day to those whose names we whisper in our hearts and minister to them according to their needs and Thy loving kindness.

Help those who are in trouble.

Give Thy consolation to those who sorrow and Thy love to us all.

In Thy name we pray. Amen.

FRIDAY, APRIL 2, 1948

O God, who hast made of one blood all the nations of mankind, so that all are kinsmen, forgive the selfishness that ignores the ties which Thou hast established.

We pray today for the people of Italy that they may be guided in the grave decisions they shortly must make.

May Thy will be done in that ancient land.

Save Thy people there from intimidation and coercion,

and give them the courage of true faith in democracy that
they may be free.

May we in this free land esteem more highly our liberties,
in the light of the price others are called upon to pay. For
Jesus' sake. Amen.   TUESDAY, APRIL 6, 1948

O GOD OUR FATHER, history and experience
have given us so many evidences of Thy guidance to
nations and to individuals that we should not doubt Thy
power or Thy willingness to direct us. Give us the faith to
believe that when God wants us to do or not do any
particular thing, God finds a way of letting us know it. May
we not make it more difficult for Thee to guide us, but be
willing to be led of Thee, that Thy will may be done in us
and through us for the good of America and all mankind.
This we ask in Jesus' name. Amen.

                            WEDNESDAY, APRIL 7, 1948

OUR FATHER, in times of confusion, when men
doubt their beliefs and believe their doubts and are
victims of ideologies that seek to divide and conquer, give
to the people of this nation a true appreciation of the great
affirmations we hold in common. Let us appreciate our
agreements and have the courage and conviction to stand
up for them, that we stand united and fearless before the
world.

Direct our government that it may ever make it as hard as
possible to do wrong and as easy as possible to do right. To
that end, incline our leaders to the eternal truths Thou hast
revealed in the Bible and in Thy Son, Jesus Christ, our Lord.
Amen.   THURSDAY, APRIL 8, 1948

Our Eternal Father, whose kindness is loving and whose patience is infinite, hear us again as we pray, not because of what we say but because of the deep need that drives us to Thee.

We rest in the thought that Thy love knows no change, else it would not love us long.

We are burdened by things that do not matter, bewildered by problems of our own creation.

Thou hast made us heirs of a great heritage and trustees of priceless things, yet we forget the price that was paid for them and the eternal vigilance required to preserve them. Make us strong, O God, in conviction, with insight for our times and courage for our testing. Through Jesus Christ our Lord. Amen.

MONDAY, APRIL 12, 1948

O Christ our living Lord, Thou hast brought us to this new day and further opportunity.

Help us to work with Thee that it may be a good day with good things done.

We know that a different world cannot be built by indifferent people. May there be no apathy in this place, no lukewarmness when we should be hot.

Abide with us, O Christ, that our hearts may burn within us and our imaginations be fired with Thy passion to do God's will. Amen.

TUESDAY, APRIL 13, 1948

Our Heavenly Father, in this moment of prayer, when there is silence in this Senate Chamber, may there not be silence in Thy presence.

May our prayers be heard.

May no short circuits be made by our lack of faith, our high professions joined to low attainments, our fine words hiding shabby thoughts, or friendly faces masking cold hearts.

Out of the same old needs, conscious of the same old faults, we pray on the same old terms for new mercies and new blessings.

In the name of Jesus Christ our Lord. Amen.

WEDNESDAY, APRIL 14, 1948

IF THESE MOMENTS, O CHRIST, can be spent in honest heart-to-heart communion with Thee, and Thou wilt give us Thy Spirit, then will our whole day be changed for us, and we shall be changed for the day. Our moods will become right, and we shall be sensitized. Use these moments, O Lord, to make every thought and feeling what they ought to be, that we may be able to do things for Thy sake that we would not have done for our own or the sake of anyone else. Amen.

THURSDAY, APRIL 15, 1948

IT IS NOT OUR BROTHERS OR OUR FRIENDS, but it is we, O Lord, who are standing in need of prayer. Much as we would like to see this great company engaged in fervent supplication, we remember that Thou hast promised: "If any two are agreed, I will do it."

Let us not be staggered by statistics but rather by the implications of the prayers here uttered by a few. When they really move us, they can move our nation. Let us not be stumbling blocks. We ask in Jesus' name. Amen.

MONDAY, APRIL 26, 1948

O God of grace and God of glory, when we resent so many choices to make, may we remember that good character is the habit of choosing right from wrong.

Help us as a nation to see that our strongest defense lies back in home and school and church where is built the character that gives free people the power to win their freedom and to hold it. May we never forget that it is only under God that this nation or any nation can be free.

And when we have learned well this lesson, then shall we have for export more than money, even the faith and idealism for which all who love liberty will be willing to live. Amen.

FRIDAY, APRIL 30, 1948

O God our Father, come nearer to us than we have ever known and stay with us through the deliberations of this day, lest we give way to selfishness.

We pray for our country, thrust by world events into high responsibility.

May she be willing to grow up, and, with adult maturity, looking unto Thee for guidance and wisdom and courage, assume her role of leader among the nations.

So may her statesmen act and her people think that Thou canst bless her and use her.

In Jesus' name we pray. Amen.

WEDNESDAY, MAY 5, 1948

Hear us, Our Father, as we pray for a freshness of spirit to renew our faith and to brighten our hopes.

Create new warmth and love between the members of

77

the Senate and those who work with them, that they may go at their work not head first but heart first.

May they be able to disagree without being disagreeable and to differ without being difficult.

In an atmosphere of team spirit, give them freedom to be honest without tension and frank without offense, that Thy spirit will not be driven from their midst.

This we ask in Jesus' name. Amen.

THURSDAY, MAY 6, 1948

FORGIVE US, Lord Jesus, for doing the things that make us uncomfortable and guilty when we pray.

We say that we believe in God, and yet we doubt God's promises.

We say that in God we trust, yet we worry and try to manage our own affairs.

We say that we love Thee, O Lord, and yet do not obey Thee.

We believe that Thou hast the answers to all our problems, and yet we do not consult Thee.

Forgive us, Lord, for our lack of faith and the willful pride that ignores the way, the truth, and the life. Wilt Thou reach down and change the gears within us that we may go forward with Thee. Amen.   MONDAY, MAY 10, 1948

O GOD OUR FATHER, be real to each one of us today, that we may become aware how near Thou art and how practical Thy help may be. Deliver us from going through the motions as though waiting for a catastrophe.

Save us from the inertia of futility.

Revive our spirit of adventuresome faith.

78

Give us nerve again and zest for living, with courage for the difficulties of peace.

Through Jesus Christ our Lord. Amen.

OUR HEAVENLY FATHER, when we have prayed for guidance and it comes, let us not think it strange if it be something we would not have thought of, for Thy thoughts are not our thoughts and our way is not Thine.

Make us eager to know Thy will and Thy way of dealing with situations, rather than devising our own plans and asking Thee to bless them. Then shall we discover how much better is Thy way and how happy they are who walk in it. Through Jesus Christ our Lord. Amen.

O LORD OUR GOD, refresh us with Thy spirit to quicken our thinking and make us sensitive to Thy will.

We may be unconscious of our deepest needs, accustomed to things as they are, ceasing to desire any changes.

We may be unwilling to pay the price of better things.

Show us, Thy servants, the things that must be changed, that we hinder Thee no more. Amen.

OUR FATHER IN HEAVEN, humbly we bow in prayer this day feeling the deep loss of our nation and the Senate in the call that has summoned our brother onto that life where age shall not weary or the years condemn.

Knowing in whom he placed his trust, we know that his faith was well founded.

We pray for those who loved him best and will miss him most. May they have the comforting ministry of Him who shall wipe away all tears from their eyes and is able to bind up broken hearts.

So teach us to number our days that we may apply our hearts unto wisdom.

May our sympathies be warm and real, and in our great loss may we learn better how to love one another, through Him who has promised, *Whoever liveth and believeth in Me shall never die. Because I live, ye shall live also.* Amen.

FRIDAY, MAY 14, 1948

O GOD, at this moment the senators and the representatives of the people of this nation humbly implore Thy help and guidance. Make it a sacred moment, a moment when men are aware of their need of God, a moment when answers come and guidance is given. Often we pray for that which is already ours, neglected and unused. Sometimes we pray for that which can never be ours and sometimes for that which we must do for ourselves.

How many times we never pray at all, and then work ourselves to death to earn something that is ours for the asking.

Help us to understand that faith without works is dead and works without faith can never live. Amen.

MONDAY, MAY 17, 1948

O LORD, in the midst of great activity today we ask Thee to remind us often of Thine invisible presence, that out of confused issues may come simplicity of plan; out of fear may come confidence; out of hurry may come the willingness to wait; out of frustration, rest and power.

This we ask in Thine own name. Amen.

O LORD OUR GOD, while dealing honestly with things as they are, keep alive our hope that things may yet be better than they are. "Earth shall be fair and all her people one: Not till that hour shall God's whole will be done."

Give us faith to believe in the possibility of change, that, each in his own place, we may do all we can to change from bad to good, and from good to better, until thou art satisfied with our labors. In the name of Jesus Christ our Lord. Amen.

OUR FATHER IN HEAVEN, today we pray for Thy gift of contentment, that we may not waste our time desiring more, but learn to use and enjoy what we have.

We may not know everything, but we may know Thee and Thy will. We need not be rich to be generous, nor have all wisdom to be understanding. Our influence may not be great, but it can be good. Our speech may not be eloquent, but it can be truthful and sincere. We cannot all have good looks, but we can have good conscience, and, having that, we shall have peace of mind and need fear no man.

May we be kind one to another, tender-hearted, forgiving one another, even as Thou, for Christ's sake, hast forgiven us. Amen.

Our Father, sometimes we are discouraged and disappointed in the government of this nation, and the common people of other lands, hungry for peace, cannot understand the difference between what we say and what we do.

We have an uneasy feeling that we have not been right or consistent and have risked the peace of the world for lesser gains at home. Only if Thy Spirit guide our spokesmen and shape our policies can this nation regain the respect of the world and merit Thy blessing. Winning peace in the world must become more important than winning votes in America.

God, direct our senators to do what is right for Jesus' sake and the sake of peace and good conscience. Amen.

TUESDAY, MAY 25, 1948

O Lord our God, have pity upon us, who have so little pity in our hearts.

We give, but not in kindness.

We give because the sound of crying disturbs us and we want to be free to look after things that concern ourselves.

We want peace without pain and security without sacrifice.

We had to accept the responsibilities of war, but we do not want to accept the responsibilities of peace.

O Lord, be patient with us.

Give us yet more time to learn what love is, and how love should act, and how love can change us as individuals and as a nation.

We pray in the name of Him who loves us all. Amen.

WEDNESDAY, MAY 26, 1948

LORD JESUS, as Thou dost move among people and see what men are doing today, how sore must be Thy heart.

Thou whose head was cradled in straw must often reflect that straw was not as coarse as man's selfishness.

Thou whose hands were spread upon a cross and fastened with nails must often reflect that nails were never so sharp as man's ingratitude.

Hear us as we pray for this poor blundering world, in which the nations never seem to learn to live as brothers.

They resort again and again to methods that produce only more bitter tears, methods that only add to misery and subtract nothing from problems.

Heal them that need healing, make strong the wavering, guide the perplexed, befriend the lonely, give new faith and courage to those whose spirits are low.

Lift up our heads, put a new light in our eyes and a new song in our hearts, and we will do better and be better for the sake of Thy love. Amen.

THURSDAY, MAY 27, 1948

SPIRIT OF GOD, come into our hearts and make us sensitive to the sufferings of other people. We think of the victims of flood and mishap and all those who have heavy hearts today. May we so grow in grace that the sympathy we feel for friends may also be felt for strangers.

Cultivate within us the grace of thankful, uncomplaining hearts; the grace of boldness on standing for what is right; the grace of self-discipline; the grace to treat others as we would have others treat us; the grace of silence, that we may refrain from hasty speech; the grace of kindness, that wherever we go we may take something of the love of God.

Be with our senators this day and bless them. We ask in Jesus' name. Amen.

TUESDAY, JUNE 1, 1948

O LORD, let us never be afraid of a new idea or unreceptive to a new thought, lest we pull down the shades of our minds and exclude Thy holy light. When confronted by mystery, help us to remember that we do not have to explain all we know or understand all we believe. But give us the grace of humility and the spirit of the open mind, the courage to persist in face of difficulties, and a steady confidence in the power of truth.

Help us all to learn something this day, that we shall be wise at its close and more ready for our eternal home when we are one step nearer.

Through Jesus Christ our Lord. Amen.

WEDNESDAY, JUNE 2, 1948

OUR FATHER IN HEAVEN, as we pray for Thy blessings upon the members of the Senate, we are not unmindful of those in the gallery who join us in this prayer. We give Thee thanks for the youth of America, the leaders of tomorrow, the young people who shall someday take our places. We thank Thee for their faith in America and we pray that nothing done or said in this place shall cause them to think any less of the institutions we cherish. Challenge them, we pray Thee, with the vision of good citizenship and a love for all that is good in America and a desire to make it even better, that this land that we love

84

may become in truth and in fact God's own country. Amen.

LORD, we are ashamed that money and position speak to us more loudly than does the simple compassion of the human heart. Help us to care, as Thou dost care, for the little people who have no lobbyists, for the minority groups who sorely need justice. May it be the glory of our government that not only the strong are heard, but also the weak; not only the powerful, but the helpless; not only those with influence, but also those who have nothing but a case and an appeal.

May we put our hearts into our work, that our work may get into our hearts. Amen.

O LORD OUR GOD, deliver us from the fear of what might happen and give us the grace to enjoy what now is and to keep striving after what ought to be. Through Jesus Christ our Lord. Amen.

O GOD, the light of those who seek Thee, grant to our minds that illumination without which we walk in darkness and know not whither we go. Remember those who feel no need of Thee, who seem content with a careless, unexamined life, whose hearts are unvisited by desires of better things. Leave them not to themselves, lest they go down to destruction. Remember us, O Lord, who do not always remember Thee, and help us to accomplish our tasks without tension or strain, that we may do good work and merit Thy blessing. For Jesus' sake. Amen.

WEDNESDAY, JUNE 9, 1948

OUR FATHER IN HEAVEN, every day we are reminded how fragile is the thread of our lives and how suddenly we may be summoned away from the things that engross us here.

May the uncertainty of life make us the more anxious to do good while we have opportunity, for the sake of the record that has eternal implications far beyond the next election.

Since we shall be judged for every idle word, let us speak carefully, with a deep respect for the truth that cannot be twisted.

Bless each member of this body, as Thou seest their needs—those who are prevented by duty elsewhere from joining in this prayer and those who appear to be so adequate for their tasks but who need Thy help like the rest of us.

Reveal Thy love to all of us and grant us Thy peace. Through Jesus Christ our Lord. Amen.

THURSDAY, JUNE 10, 1948

HELP US, OUR FATHER, to show other nations an America to imitate—not the America of loud jazz music, self-seeking indulgence, and love of money, but the America that loves fair play, honest dealing, straight talk, real freedom, and faith in God.

Make us to see that it cannot be done as long as we are content to be coupon clippers on the original investment made by our forefathers. Give us faith in God and love for our fellow men, that we may have something to deposit on which the young people of today can draw interest tomorrow.

By Thy grace, let us this day increase the moral capital of this country. Amen.

FRIDAY, JUNE 11, 1948

LORD JESUS, as we pray for the members of this body, its officers, and all those who share in its labors, we remember that Thou wert never in a hurry and never lost Thine inner peace even under pressure greater than we shall ever know.

But we are only human.

We grow tired.

We feel the strain of meeting deadlines, and we chafe under frustration.

We need poise and peace of mind, and only Thou canst supply the deepest needs of tired bodies, jaded spirits, and frayed nerves.

Give to us Thy peace and refresh us in our weariness, that this may be a good day with much done and done well, that we may say with Thy servant Paul, "I can do all things through Christ, who gives me strength." Amen.

SATURDAY, JUNE 12, 1948

ETERNAL GOD, who hast made us and designed us for companionship with Thee, who hast called us to walk with Thee and be not afraid, forgive us, we pray Thee, if fear, unworthy thought, or hidden sin has prompted us to hide from Thee.

87

Save us, we pray, from all sins of intellect, not only from the error and ignorance which belong to our frailty, but from the pride that would make us think ourselves sufficient for our tasks.

Forgive us for thinking of prayer as a waste of time, and help us to see that without it our labors are a waste of effort.

O God, help us, guide us, and use us for Thy glory and our good. Through Jesus Christ our Lord. Amen.

MONDAY, JUNE 14, 1948

O GOD OUR FATHER, in these days when men freely judge and condemn each other, remind us all of the Great Assize before which we must all someday appear.

Thou knowest whether we have been voices or merely echoes, whether we have done Thy will or our own or, worse still, have done neither.

Teach us, O Lord, that only Thy "Well done" will afford peace and everlasting happiness.

May we strive for that rather than the approval of men, which is but for a little while. In Jesus' name we pray. Amen.

FRIDAY, JUNE 18, 1948

O GOD, our Father, may the year that is past teach us and not torment.

Help us to be realistic about ourselves.

May we not steal credit for success, nor deny blame for failure. Give us the grace to take things as they are, and to resolve, by Thy help, to make them what they ought to be, in the strong name of Jesus Christ our Lord. Amen.

FRIDAY, DECEMBER 31, 1948

EIGHTY-FIRST CONGRESS
FIRST SESSION

O LORD OUR GOD, look with favor upon the members of the Senate, and bless each one of them according to his needs. May they be aware of a mandate higher than that of a ballot box, a mandate from Thee, to legislate wisely and well. We believe that Thou wilt accept these men as representatives of the people, and art willing to work in them and through them that they may become instruments of Thy will. Grant that they be willing to have it so, through Jesus Christ our Lord, who taught us to pray together:

Our Father which art in heaven, hallowed be Thy name. Thy kingdom come. Thy will be done in earth as it is in heaven. Give us this day our daily bread. And forgive us our debts as we forgive our debtors. And lead us not into temptation, but deliver us from evil: for Thine is the kingdom, and the power, and the glory, for ever,

Amen. MONDAY, JANUARY 3, 1949

OUR FATHER IN HEAVEN, give us the long view of our work and our world.

Help us to see that it is better to fail in a cause that will ultimately succeed than to succeed in a plan that will ultimately fail.

Guide us how to work and then teach us how to wait.

O Lord, we pray in the name of Jesus, who was never in a
hurry. Amen. WEDNESDAY, JANUARY 5, 1949

IN THIS PRAYER, O God, we come to Thee as
children to a loving Father. We pray that Thou wilt
help our senators to face the problems that confront them,
not alone by giving them wisdom greater than their own, but
also by relieving their minds of all other anxieties. May they
now turn over to Thee loved ones who need the healing
touch of the Great Physician, with every confidence that
Thou wilt hear our prayers of intercession, and as we do the
work that is before us, Thou wilt do Thy work of healing in
those whom we love. May Thy help be so plain and practical
in our family affairs that we shall come to believe strongly in
the help Thou dost offer in our national affairs.

Deliver Thy servants from personal worries, that they
may be able to give themselves wholly to the challenges of
this hour. In Jesus' name we ask it. Amen.

THURSDAY, JANUARY 6, 1949

OUR FATHER, since we cannot always do what we
like, grant that we may like what we must do, knowing
that truth will one day be vindicated and right in the end
must prevail.

Bless thy servants this day and keep them all in Thy
peace. Amen. MONDAY, JANUARY 10, 1949

STOP US, O GOD, for a minute of prayer.
Stop our anxious minds from wandering, and our
hearts from desiring anything but to know Thy will.

Let us stand at attention before Thee and hear what Thou hast to say to us.

We believe that Thou canst tell us not only what to do, but also how to do it.

If it needs making up our minds, Thou who didst make our minds canst show us how to make them up.

If it needs changing our minds, Thou canst work that miracle, too.

Speak, O Lord, and make us hear, for Jesus' sake. Amen.

THURSDAY, JANUARY 13, 1949

HELP US, O GOD, to treat every human heart as if it were breaking, and to consider the feeling of others as we do our own.

Help us to be gentle, and to control our tempers that we may learn to love one another. Give us the grace so to live this day, in the name of Jesus, who loves us all. Amen.

MONDAY, JANUARY 17, 1949

OUR FATHER IN HEAVEN, once again we offer unto Thee our grateful thanks for Thy mercy that cared for us during the night and brought us safely to this hour.

Today is the tomorrow we worried about yesterday, and we see how foolish our anxiety was.

Teach us to trust Thee more completely and to seek Thy help in all that we have to do, through Jesus Christ, our Lord. Amen.

TUESDAY, JANUARY 18, 1949

GOD OF OUR FATHERS, in whom we trust, and by whose guidance and grace this nation was born, bless the senators of these United States at this important time in history and give them all things needful to the faithful discharge of their responsibilities.

We pray especially today for our President, and also for him who will preside over this Chamber.

Give to them good health for the physical strains of their office, good judgment for the decisions they must make, wisdom beyond their own, and clear understanding for the problems of this difficult hour.

We thank Thee for their humble reliance upon Thee. May they go often to the throne of grace, as we commend them both to Thy loving care and Thy guiding hand. Through Jesus Christ our Saviour. Amen.

THURSDAY, JANUARY 20, 1949

TODAY, O LORD, as the members of the Senate pause in this moment of prayer, we unite our petitions for Thy blessing upon Thy servant who, in his new capacity, presides over this body. We thank Thee for his long years of devoted public service, for the testimony of his life and the inspiration of his example.

May he never feel lonely in this chair, but always be aware of Thy hand upon him and Thy spirit with him.

When differences arise, as they will, may Thy servants be not disturbed at being misunderstood, but rather be disturbed at not understanding.

May Thy will be done here, and may Thy program be carried out, above party and personality, beyond time and circumstance, for the good of America and the peace of the world. Through Jesus Christ our Lord. Amen.

MONDAY, JANUARY 24, 1949

Resolved, That the Senate has heard with profound sorrow and regret of the death of Reverend Peter Marshall, doctor of divinity, late the Chaplain of the Senate.

—Senate Resolution No. 43
Eighty-First Congress, First Session
(Submitted by Mr. Lucas)
In the Senate of the United States
Attest: Leslie L. Biffle, Secretary
JANUARY 27, 1949

The Vice President. Prayer will be offered by Dr. Clarence W. Cranford, minister, Calvary Baptist Church, of Washington, D.C.

Dr. Cranford. The prayer I shall offer this morning was written for this session by Dr. Peter Marshall, as one of the last things he did before he died.

DELIVER US, OUR FATHER, from futile hopes and from clinging to lost causes, that we may move into ever-growing calm and ever-widening horizons.

Where we cannot convince, let us be willing to persuade, for small deeds done are better than great deeds planned.

We know that we cannot do everything. But help us to do something. For Jesus' sake. Amen.

THURSDAY, JANUARY 27, 1949

IN MEMORIAM

PETER MARSHALL

BORN 1902, COATBRIDGE, SCOTLAND

DIED 1949, WASHINGTON, D.C.

PETER MARSHALL

—FROM THE CONGRESSIONAL
RECORD, JANUARY 27, 1949

Mr. Lucas. Mr. President, the news of the sudden and untimely death of the Reverend Peter Marshall, Chaplain of the Senate, comes as a shock to all of the members of the Senate, whose wholehearted affection and admiration he enjoyed.

In his capacity as Chaplain of the Senate, he exercised a spiritual influence and moral guidance felt by every member here. While he had no voice in determining policy and had no vote on any measure that came before us, his prayers carried a weight in our hearts and many times moved us in the right direction.

He was a man of great piety and great wit, a man with strength of soul and fine personal charm, whose memory will be bright in the recollections of every senator for many years to come.

His beautiful and eloquent prayers for the Senate were often remarked upon by members of the press, and often noted by our friends and visitors here. He put the whole power of his spirit into his beseechings of Almighty God, and he carried all of us with him.

In his youth, in Scotland, he worked with his hands in the steel mills. Later he felt the call of a religious vocation, and entered the Presbyterian ministry. He came to our country as a young man, and became a citizen of our nation to work among us as a man of God.

We honor him today as he goes to the final judgment of his Maker, to give account of his life upon this earth as a great human being, a great minister, a great American. He takes his place in the long line of distinguished Chaplains who have served the Senate.

Mr. President, I now ask unanimous consent to offer the resolution which I send to the desk and ask to have read, and I ask unanimous consent for its immediate consideration.

(There being no objection, the resolution (S. Res. 43) was read, and the Senate proceeded to its consideration:)

"Resolved, That the senate has heard with profound sorrow and regret of the death of Rev. Peter Marshall, D. D., late the Chaplain of the Senate."

Mr. Saltonstall. Mr. President, I should like to say just a few words in regard to the resolution offered by the majority leader.

The minority leader the Senator from Nebraska [Mr. Wherry] is unfortunately not able to be present here today to express his personal feelings and the feelings all of us share at the loss of our Chaplain. Peter Marshall was Senator Wherry's pastor. He officiated at the marriage of his daughter. I know he feels a great personal loss. So do we all.

Our Chaplain, Mr. Marshall, always opened our sessions with prayers that helped and inspired us all. They combined brevity with common sense. They always aptly expressed in religious terms the problems of the moment. Above all, they were inspired with deep spiritual feeling. I recall his words about the meaning of liberty:

"Teach us that liberty is not only to be loved but also to

be lived. Liberty is too precious a thing to be buried in books. It costs too much to be hoarded. Make us to see that liberty is not the right to do as we please, but the opportunity to please to do what is right."

Never shall we forget the morsels of thought that were contained in his prayers. They were replete with earthy phrases—phrases which caught the attention and made meaningful his spiritual message.

Most of us came to know our Chaplain only two short years ago. We immediately felt the impact of his prayers, so we wanted to know him better. I always found him full of humor, a man of ready repartee, and intensely human. Why shouldn't he be? He was a man who knew how to toil with his hands. He knew what it was to work hard for an education, and he had what we need so much in the world today— the inspiration to be a spiritual leader. So, with hard work and much sacrifice, he became one. We have been the beneficiaries of his toil and his inspiration. All of us will miss his daily words of guidance to us. Most of us on the day on which President Truman was inaugurated heard Dr. Marshall's prayer. It will remain in our minds as typifying the spirit of the man who said these words:

"Give to them good health for the physical strains of their office, good judgment for the decisions they must make, wisdom beyond their own, and clear understanding for the problems of this difficult hour.

"We thank Thee for their humble reliance upon Thee. May they go often to the throne of grace, as we commend them both to Thy loving care and Thy guiding hand. Amen."

These words and the memory of the man who said them will remain long with us.

Mr. Kefauver. Mr. President, at a time like this words are of little consequence. Peter Marshall has made his record and it is indeed a brilliant one. A man above politics, he bowed to the needs and desires of this body. Would that God give all of us here in the Senate the strength and courage to live up to his simple, provocative yet easily understood prayers.

Peter Marshall was not born in this great land of ours. He was a native of Scotland, a nation that has sent many of her sons to our shores, who have made a real contribution to our democratic way of life. Peter Marshall was indeed among that illustrious group.

His early life was not an easy one. Working with his fellow man in the every-day world before becoming a minister of the Gospel, he pursued the same hard road many others have taken. Yet he remained the same unaffected man he had always been. Upon attaining what many of us would call a highly successful status, but with which he would disagree, Peter Marshall did not forget those he might have met along the way. As a Scotsman, his creed might well be expressed in a verse from Robert Burns of whom Peter Marshall was an ardent admirer:

THEN LET US PRAY THAT COME IT MAY,
    AS COME IT WILL FOR A' THAT,
THAT SENSE AND WORTH O'ER A' THE EARTH,
    SHALL BEAR THE GREE[1] AND A' THAT;
FOR A' THAT AND A' THAT
    ITS COMIN' YET FOR A' THAT
THAT MAN TO MAN, THE WORLD O'ER
    SHALL BRITHERS BE FOR A' THAT.

[1] Have the prize.

Mr. Bridges. Mr. President, I present a resolution adopted by the Republican minority conference today. This resolution was submitted to the conference by me on behalf of the Senator from Nebraska [Mr. Wherry], and I ask unanimous consent that it may be printed at this point in the Record.

(There being no objection, the resolution was ordered to be printed in the Record, as follows:)

"Whereas Almighty God in His infinite wisdom has taken from the United States Senate its beloved Chaplain, the Reverend Peter Marshall; and

"Whereas he has rendered to the membership of the United States Senate through his daily prayers a spiritual service of great and lasting value; and

"Whereas he was our affectionate friend, ever ready to give of himself, of his efforts, and of his judgment for our guidance in the ways of righteousness and Christian living: Now, therefore, be it

"Resolved, That we, the Republican members of the United States Senate, express our loss at his passing; and be it further

"Resolved, That a copy of this resolution be transmitted to Mrs. Catherine Marshall that she may be assured of our deep sympathy and condolences upon the passing of our friend her husband."

Mr. Bridges. Mr. President, I also ask unanimous consent to have printed in the Record two editorials, one from the Washington Post of January 26, 1949, and the other from the Washington Evening Star of January 26, 1949, paying deserved tribute to the late Chaplain of the Senate, Dr. Peter Marshall.

(There being no objections, the editorials were ordered to be printed in the Record, as follows:)

Peter Marshall

We deplore, as the Capital must, the untimely death of Dr. Peter Marshall, the 46-year-old Chaplain of the Senate who was also pastor of the New York Avenue Presbyterian Church. Till Dr. Marshall came to the Senate 2 years ago, the senators had heard a more or less perfunctory sort of "grace" before they began their deliberations. The Presbyterian minister opened the ears of the bowed senators to his words of prayer, and he put those words alongside their subsequent speeches. They were novel out of the mouth of a minister, pointed in their application to the business in hand, and charged with an hortatory spirit that carried conviction. His voice had a vibrancy, his words a Scot's tang, his presence a manliness, that enabled his allocution to linger in the senatorial memory. Only recently an American citizen, having been born in Scotland, he had a passion for America. His zest for life was as fresh and as real as his religion. He inspired the younger generation with sermons that, while without profundity, brought a living God into their lives. His is a loss that the Senate will not easily repair and that his growing congregation can ill spare.

[FROM THE WASHINGTON POST
OF JANUARY 26, 1949]

Dr. Peter Marshall

Living and working in Washington only eleven years, the Reverend Dr. Peter Marshall nevertheless has left his mark upon the whole city. He was a man of contagious spirit, eager and alert, quick to see opportunities of service and to meet their challenge. Within a few months after coming here he had made himself an influence throughout the entire community. Wherever he went, whatever he did, the result of his presence was constructive. In classic language, he was a builder of the Kingdom of God on this earth.

Perhaps one explanation of Dr. Marshall's power might be found in the fact that he was a son of the people and kept his touch with them even when he had risen to high station. Born and reared against a bleak and uncongenial background, he earned his bread as a laborer in his youth. His formal education was limited to a mechanical and mining college at Coatbridge in Scotland and the Columbia Seminary at Decatur in Georgia. Most of his scholarly achievement he owed to his inquiring mind. The magic of his eloquence was a native gift which he shared with Burns and Carlyle, Hugh Miller and John Buchan. But he was a great preacher because of an inner genius, a force of faith which demanded expression in human ministry.

His decade at the New York Avenue Presbyterian Church was a period of progress which soon will find fulfillment in a new religious center on the site long ago hallowed by the presence of Abraham Lincoln. Dr. Marshall will not see the building program finished, but his association with its start will be an asset always. He is certain of remembrance, too, at the Capitol. Able interpreters of the Word preceded him in the chaplaincy of the Senate, and he contributed notably to the tradition which they established. His final prayer for government "above party and personality, beyond time and circumstance, for the good of America and the peace of the world" was a masterful utterance which well may be regarded as his testament to the country he adopted and dearly loved.

[FROM THE WASHINGTON EVENING
STAR OF JANUARY 26, 1949]

Peter Marshall

Mr. Magnuson. Mr. President, on Tuesday, January 25, we received word that Peter Marshall, our Senate Chaplain, had died. All of us who knew him were shocked and grieved.

During the 2 years Peter Marshall served as Chaplain of the Senate each of us came to know, respect, and revere him. From his words we drew counsel and guidance.

Peter Marshall's influence in the United States Senate extended to the Press and Radio Galleries.

Mr. Tris Coffin devoted his column of January 28 to an appreciation of Peter Marshall. I ask unanimous consent to place in the Appendix of the Record Tris Coffin's column, The Daybook. Further I recommend that each senator and member of the galleries read this tribute to Peter Marshall.

(There being no objection, the article was ordered to be printed in the Record, as follows:)

[FROM THE CONGRESSIONAL
RECORD, JANUARY 31, 1949]

The Daybook

BY TRIS COFFIN

The clear voice with the faint Scotch burr sounded across the dim and gloomy Chamber, ". . . May Thy will be done here and Thy program be carried out above party and personality, beyond time and circumstance, for the good of America and the peace of the world."

The Senators sat quietly, a little humbled as they always were by the sincerity of the young Chaplain. These were the last words spoken by Peter Marshall in the United States Senate. He died the next morning, a man who had lived a full and rewarding life, at 46.

Dr. Marshall, a Scotch Presbyterian, was the conscience of the Senate. His voice was soft and gentle, but his words cut cleanly through the pompousness and demagoguery on Capitol Hill. He told this correspondent wistfully one morning, "The Senators may not want me long for their chaplain, but I must speak out."

One of his admirers, Senator Harley Kilgore, of West Virginia, spoke of him in awe: "Peter Marshall expresses more feeling and says more in his short prayers than all the Senators put together the rest of the day."

Dr. Marshall's belief in human rights was a passion so deep it glowed in his face and burned in his words. Yet he was a soft-spoken man who had no use for cheap dramatics. He spoke honestly of what was on his mind, and that was all. He died at 46 because he devoted all his energies to helping others.

Everything Peter Marshall did, he did with great care. In his small, old-fashioned office in the New York Avenue Presbyterian Church, Dr. Marshall worked for hours over his short daily prayer in the Senate.

One of the great documents of recent times was Peter Marshall's Fourth of July sermon 2 years ago. It was reproduced in the Congressional Record. Fifty thousand copies were mailed out on request.

The young pastor said: "The freedom that was purchased 171 years ago was not paid for in one down payment. Installments have been kept up for more than two lifetimes, for this is one possession that exacts a perpetual price. There is a danger in your sitting back smugly applauding when the flag is thrown upon the movie screen, puffing yourself up with pride, as you boast of America. For you were free-born.

"Unless you have lived in other lands, unless you have known hunger and persecution, unless you have come as an immigrant to this good land, you have no idea how good it is. Nor can you truly be grateful, since you have no conception of what it means to be without all things you take for granted.

"You have never known anything else. It is because they who went before you were willing to stake their lives, their fortunes, and their sacred honor, that you have what you now enjoy. But you forget how bitterly it was won.

"The story of the waste of this country's resources is a sad story of greed and selfishness. The wildlife of this nation has long been exploited to satisfy the greed and so-called sporting instinct of free Americans. That same kind of greed was shown in our treatment of the land.

"It was a good land, but we were greedy. We wanted money crops, and the slogan was, 'Plow and plant, plow and plant.' We moved on when the land gave out. Our reckless stripping away of the vegetable cover of the soil has driven out the animals and invited erosion.

"The same wanton waste and disregard for the future is to be seen in the almost criminal waste of oil; in the deforestation of our country, when the slogan seemed to be, 'Cut and sell, cut and sell.' Surely freedom does not mean that people can do what they like with the country's resources. The natural resources of America are the heritage of the whole nation, and should be conserved and utilized for the benefit of all people.

"It is time we put Bible back into our government; time that our statesmen began to make their decisions on all moral questions on the basis of the authority of God's holy word. It is only by applying Christ's solutions to the problems that plague us, it is only by living under His blessing and guidance, that we can ever hope to add any glory to Old Glory."

[FROM THE WASHINGTON (D.C.)
TIMES-HERALD OF JANUARY 28, 1949]

Peter Marshall

The Vice President. The Chair lays before the Senate a certified copy of prefatory remarks made by the chaplain of the Ohio State Senate regarding the death of Rev. Peter Marshall, late the Chaplain of the United States Senate, which, without objection, will be printed in the Record.

(There being no objection, the remarks were ordered to be printed in the Record, as follows:)

"The United States Senate is without a Chaplain. A brilliant life came suddenly to an end yesterday in Washington. The Reverend Peter Marshall has had a distinguished career as Chaplain of the Senate, if my information is correct, following that of the late Dr. ZeBarney T. Phillips, of Springfield, Ohio. He was popular with the senators, being as he was an outspokenly honest man who challenged them constantly to be outstanding leaders in the high office to which the American people had elected them. He was pastor of the New York Avenue Presbyterian Church, where Abraham Lincoln worshiped while President of this great nation. We shall remember him and his loved ones in their bereavement today in our prayer:

"'In the midst of life we are in death; of whom may we seek for succor, but of Thee, O Lord, who for our sins art justly displeased?'"

Let us pray:

"O God whose days are without end and whose mercies cannot be numbered, accept our prayers on behalf of the soul of Thy servant departed and grant him an entrance into the love of life and joy, in the fellowship of Thy saints. Defend the members of his bereaved family with Thy heavenly grace that they may continue Thine forever and daily increase in Thy Holy Spirit more and more until they too come into Thine everlasting Kingdom.

"May the souls of the faithful by the mercies of God rest in peace.

"May he rest in peace." Amen.

This is to certify that this is a true and correct copy of prefatory remarks made by the Rev. John I. Byron, chaplain, Ohio State Senate, Columbus, Ohio, January 26, 1949, regarding the death of Rev. Peter Marshall, Chaplain of the United States Senate, Washington, D. C.

Dwight L. Matchette,
Clerk of the Senate.

[FROM THE CONGRESSIONAL RECORD, FEBRUARY 3, 1949]

Mr. O'Conor. Mr. President, on the occasion of a recent meeting of the Senate eulogies were expressed by different members of the Senate concerning the life and work of the late Peter Marshall, Chaplain of the Senate, whose recent untimely death has been mourned by us all.

Because I was engaged in a committee meeting at the time when these eulogies were being expressed, opportunity was not given for me to voice my sentiments in regard to Dr. Marshall's noble character, integrity, and attractive personality.

I therefore ask unanimous consent to have inserted in the body of the Congressional Record a statement expressive of my innermost feelings in tribute to his memory.

(There being no objection, the statement was ordered to be printed in the Record, as follows:)

Rev. Peter Marshall

With other members of the Senate and countless friends of our late Chaplain, I was profoundly shocked and grieved to receive the news of his untimely death.

The splendid influence for good which he exerted, the high ideals which were voiced by him in his invocations, and his noble example all combined to stamp him first as a man of God and secondly, as a man among men.

I am prompted to express myself because of a unique experience which I had with Dr. Marshall only very recently. Since the beginning of our session earlier this month, death has taken from our family one who was cherished and loved most tenderly. As soon as this event occurred, he brought comfort and consolation to other members of the family and to me by a very sympathetic message. Later, upon my return to the Senate, he made a special point to give personally a most heartening expression of condolence.

His words to me now appear to have been almost prophetic. Emphasizing the fact that life on earth is merely a temporary sojourn, he asserted that all are striving for the same goal although our course may be along various denominational paths.

While little did he think that he himself was so near to death, his comments on the value of faith in a supernatural life could not help but leave a lasting impression. I can but repeat, in expressing hope for the happy repose of his soul, the very words which he used in commenting upon my bereavement, "May our Lord comfort and give peace."

Dr. Marshall's good works and noble endeavors will be the best monument to him which can be treasured by all who knew him. I express the sentiments of others with whom I have spoken concerning our late Chaplain in tribute to his memory by quoting the lines of the poet:

> OUT OF THE STRAIN OF THE DOING
> INTO THE PEACE OF THE DONE
> OUT OF THE THIRST OF PURSUING
> INTO THE RAPTURE WON
> OUT OF PALE DUSK INTO DAWN
> OUT OF ALL WRONG INTO RIGHTNESS
> WE FROM THESE FIELDS SHALL BE GONE
> "NAY" SAY THE SAINTS, "NOT GONE BUT COME
> INTO ETERNITY'S HARVEST HOME."

[FROM THE CONGRESSIONAL
RECORD, FEBRUARY 10, 1949]